ALIVE IN

Alive in the Spirit

A biblical and practical guide

Rob Warner

Hodder & Stoughton
LONDON SYDNEY AUCKLAND

Copyright © Rob Warner 1997

First published in Great Britain 1997

10 9 8 7 6 5 4 3 2 1

British Library Cataloguing in Publication Data
A record for this book is available from the British Library

ISBN 0 340 64197 5

Typeset by Hewer Text Composition Services, Edinburgh
Printed and bound in Great Britain by
Cox & Wyman Ltd, Reading, Berks.

Hodder and Stoughton Ltd
A Division of Hodder Headline PLC
338 Euston Road
London NW1 3BH

To Norman and Margaret
a spiritual father and mother to many

The Christian Ministry Series

As a publisher I had the privilege of publishing the I Believe Series and the Jesus Library. It is an even greater privilege to be the editor for this new series, designed to equip the local church for effective ministry in the new millennium. The Christian Ministry Series will contain books on a wide range of local church ministries. Every author will be asked to provide a bedrock of stimulating biblical reflection, combined with a practical approach to help that particular dimension of ministry really take off in the local church. The series is committed to excellence, with each title produced by a prominent leader in their field. My prayer is that these books will release *maximum ministry* in many churches around the world.

While some will discover the series as a result of those books that deal with their particular specialist ministries, we hope that many will decide that the growing series is a resource that they cannot afford to be without. The Christian Ministry Series will help them to develop and improve their present ministry but also enable them to branch out into areas they have never explored before. We also believe that many local churches, as well as individual leaders, will recognise the value of collecting the entire series, whether to add to an existing range of resources or to begin such an investment in resources for effective ministry.

Rob Warner
Queen's Road Church
Wimbledon

Contents

Preface

My first book on the Holy Spirit was written while I was training for the ministry at Regent's Park College, within the University of Oxford. Previously I had been responsible for the Christian books division at Hodder and Stoughton, where my authors included Michael Green and David Watson. Among his many books, Michael had written a very significant study of the Holy Spirit with which he had launched the I Believe Series, surely the most influential evangelical series of the seventies and eighties. Michael is an evangelist as well as a theologian, and among his widely read evangelistic books was one entitled *You Must Be Joking*, which tackled head on the most popular excuses for avoiding Jesus. I discussed with him the possibility of a companion book that would in a similar way refute Christians' popular excuses for avoiding the Holy Spirit. Michael was very supportive of the project, and encouraged me to find the ideal author. It looked as if David Watson was that man.

David had originally been sent to York to assist in the closure of a dying church, but under his ministry that church had been turned around. Eventually the congregation moved to another nearly redundant building in the centre of York, St Michael-le-Belfrey, which in turn became filled with believers and the presence of God. During David's ministry at St Michael's, I was fortunate enough to attend that church while studying English at the University of York. David's preaching and the life and growth of the church were for me a revolutionary inspiration. During my time at St Michael's, David prayed for me to be filled with the Holy Spirit, and my call to full-time ministry was confirmed.

David's first book for Hodder had been *One in the Spirit*. A gracious and gentle introduction to the work of the Spirit, it had originally been written for another publisher, but David had transferred to Hodder when he eventually became exasperated with their inordinate capacity for caution and their continued requests for further toning down of his teaching. Several years after its initial publication, David was very sympathetic to my suggestion that the time had come for a revised edition, in which, as a result of the continued advance of renewal, he would be free to be less circumspect and develop his teaching more fully. When we first met to discuss the project, David was willing to take it on. Cancer was diagnosed not long after, and so he never did have time for that particular book, devoting his last energies as a writer to *Fear No Evil*, his remarkable and courageous account of facing death through terminal cancer.

After I had left Hodder, my successors approached me about the possibility of writing a similar book myself. Time was tight around my academic studies, but I calculated that I could give a limited number of weeks to the project during vacation time, so that it would not collide with my university commitments or pastoral training. The book was completed on schedule, and to my great delight was published while I was still at Oxford and even ascended the Christian bestsellers' list. In recent years, as I have increasingly travelled around the country speaking at conferences, town- and city-wide celebrations, leaders' meetings and local churches, I have been very encouraged by the number of leaders who have expressed their appreciation for *Rediscovering the Spirit*. Their repeated requests for a revised edition have spurred me on to the task of writing this new book.

More than a decade since I first wrote on the Holy Spirit, my evangelical and charismatic convictions have not changed. Rather, they have grown stronger, for it is only with the truth of God's Word and in the power of the Holy Spirit that we can hope to see true spiritual renewal in local churches, and beyond renewal look to the possibility of revival in the Western world. In these years I have been able to learn something about introducing and strengthening renewal in the local church, not least through my own mistakes, and so one of the new dimensions in this book is a greater emphasis on the practicalities of local church renewal. I also see more clearly the connections between the Spirit and revival and the foundational importance of an unreserved commitment to developing a thoroughgoing integration of the Word and the Spirit. I hope that those who used to recommend the previous book to others as a biblical and practical introduction to the work of the Spirit will find this to be a worthy successor. At the same time I trust that the new material will leave those who bought the original book with no regrets at buying *Alive in the Spirit*. I have enjoyed writing this book enormously, and I pray that its impact will be very great indeed, both for many individual Christians and for many local churches.

My particular thanks go to Queen's Road Church Wimbledon, where Claire and I are able to experience what it means to live in the Spirit. We are so grateful for the privilege of belonging to this church, and for all the support that makes my travelling and writing ministry possible. Claire, James and Tom have been patient and supportive while I have been writing, and I'm also very thankful to my fellow elders, Norman, Malcolm, Keith, Ian, Gordon and Colin, to my support team who keep me on the road, Debbie, Margaret, Alison and Olive. Thanks must also go to the churches which first showed me renewal in action – St Michael-le-Belfrey, Ichthus and Banbury Baptist Church – and also to the two churches where I was able to learn about Spirit-filled ministry in the hot seat of pastoral leadership, Buckhurst Hill and Herne Hill Baptist Churches. Spring Harvest and Mainstream are gratefully thanked for providing many opportunities for my understanding of Word and Spirit to grow. I am also grateful for my Apple laptop which has accompanied me on many preaching trips and has always performed reliably, from Copenhagen to Plymouth, from Newcastle to Paris. I am so grateful to those who have patiently received and encouraged my teaching and writing ministries over the years.

ROB WARNER
Pentecost 1996

DISCOVERING THE SPIRIT

1

Longing for more

When I was a young Christian, the Holy Spirit had me confused. In one Bible study on Acts chapter 2, the group leader said, 'Let's not talk about the Holy Spirit. It's too controversial!' I didn't know much about the Spirit, but I knew that if he was important in the New Testament, he should be important to me.

Paul clearly stated in Romans 8:9 that every believer receives the Spirit at conversion. But when I was converted no one said anything more than that. Church leaders made it clear that beliefs need to be based on the sure foundation of Scripture, not on what I happen to feel today. They warned me not to trust emotions, and seemed to rule out any talk about experiencing the Spirit in that dangerous emotional category. Emotionalism means putting emotions in charge of beliefs and making them sovereign over Scripture – if I don't feel something is true today, then it isn't. Emotionalism means trying to use God like a spiritual Valium, a religious 'happiness pill' to keep us high and carefree. I knew that such supercharged emotions could be full of sound and fury, but evaporate overnight. They quickly turn as flat as a bottle of cola with the screw top left undone.

If a VIP had visited our church I would have felt emotion. I certainly expressed emotion seeing my team win the FA Cup. If the Queen had visited the church I cannot imagine how thrilled we all would have been. And like most Englishmen I felt overwhelmed with joy when England won the World Cup. But there was little room in my faith for emotion before the sovereign of the universe, or before Jesus Christ who for us has conquered sin, death and Satan.

I could see the danger of too much emotion more clearly than the danger of too little. My faith and understanding were growing, but were too theoretical, too head-centred. I would probably have doubted the 'soundness' of many enthusiastic first-century Christians. Behind this fear of emotion lay a deeper fear. My wariness of charismatics was in reality an excuse. I was afraid of what the Holy Spirit might do to me, and so I tried to keep him at a distance. Hostility to emotion (itself of course emotional), suspicion of experience and fear of the Spirit were drying up the well-springs of my new-found faith.

Many Christians know this ignorance and fear of the Holy Spirit. I wasn't satisfied, and thirsted for something more. Paul explains that this is a preparatory work of the Spirit who makes us first willing and then able to fulfil God's purposes (Phil. 2:13). He encourages us to want to fit into God's ways even when our lives are out of tune with Christ. I felt stuck, with little sense of direction as a Christian. I could look back to my conversion, and know that I was now forgiven and set free by Christ. I knew that Jesus had died for me and that through God's love I had received new birth and eternal life. My life had certainly come to a new beginning, but Sunday services and sermons were growing stale and unreal.

I had lost direction, and though I knew backwards the need for salvation, hearing it over again was becoming less and less important. I didn't know what to do between new birth and paradise. I began to wish that new birth whisked you straight to heaven, like the express elevator to the viewing stages of the Eiffel Tower. The weary cry of my heart was, 'What next?' Many have told me since of a similar staleness. Many need to rediscover how Christians are meant to live. Christians in a rut need to be delivered from their weariness to rediscover the adventure of God's glorious and enthralling plans for his children. Above all, that means rediscovering the Holy Spirit. The first Christians were not bored Christians.

I also felt trapped by my own personality, because change just didn't seem possible. No matter how much effort I made, some old habits and attitudes stubbornly defied every attempt at eviction. Others seemed to disappear for a few weeks or months, only to take up residence again just when I thought I'd got rid of them. Try as I might, I couldn't get clear of the sins that stuck close. My attempts to reflect the positive love of Christ were even more hopeless. I didn't mention this struggle to anyone else. I didn't mind joining in a general confession of sin. But I was much less keen on being individually identified as a 'miserable offender'. What was more, no one else ever mentioned similar difficulties. I thought that must mean that the Christian life was as natural for them as it was unnatural for me. Maybe I was a predestined failure! I was tempted to give everything up.

If only I had confessed my difficulties to someone. Perhaps they might have told me a similar story. Not that we are always defeated as Christians, but that change is never complete or easy this side of the grave. We do have to wrestle with the power of sin, but in the power of Christ, not alone in our weakness. We need one eye on the person we used to be, to receive encouragement from any progress, and one eye on Christ, never to lose sight of how far is left to go. In my defeat, I felt like Jeremiah when he suggested that Israelites were beyond change for the better. He felt their sins were as much part of them as the spots on the leopard; and a leopard cannot change its spots: 'Can the leopard change its spots? Neither can you do good who are accustomed to doing evil' (Jer. 13:23). In our heart of hearts nothing finally changes if we are left to our own strength. When Jeremiah prophesied the new covenant, he looked forward to the power of God at work in people's hearts, changing them on the inside (Jer. 31:31–4). No one had explained this to me, and no one had told me about the continued struggle of learning to live like Jesus. It was as if the new birth brought forgiveness for the past and a clean sheet, but then it was up to you to change yourself. If only I had seen more clearly!

Jesus's promise

Jesus promised his disciples that they would never be left on their own. When he returned to the Father, another Comforter would come, who would be like Jesus and would continue his ministry through his followers (John 16:7). The Spirit would not be an optional extra, or the preserve of spiritual specialists. On the contrary, it was only by the Spirit that conversion, discipleship and the new family of Christ could become living realities.

Just as a car is not really a car unless it has an engine, Paul said that without the Spirit, all we have is outward conformity. He called this holding to the form of Christianity but denying its power (2 Tim. 3:5). The first disciples had to wait for the Spirit. They were ordinary men, without outstanding abilities. When they abandoned Jesus at his arrest, their lack of courage left them all shamefaced and Peter in tears. When Mary told them she had seen Jesus risen from the dead, their first reaction was to dismiss it as foolish women's talk. But it was these men whom Jesus had chosen to turn the world upside down. Jesus didn't choose the great scholars or the religious high priests. He didn't select men of influence, in good favour with the officials of the Roman Empire. Learning and priestcraft, power and travel were far from the everyday experience of these ordinary men. Their task was to proclaim the risen Christ and build his Church throughout the world. But first they had to stay in Jerusalem. They had no inner resources which might cause them not to wait. Christ was in charge, and he would send power from on high, just as he had promised.

At the first Christian Pentecost, Peter took up this theme in a wonderful sermon. The unschooled fisherman held the crowd spellbound. When he had finished, three thousand new converts were added to the Church, on its very first day in existence. The power of the Spirit to fulfil the promises of Jesus was beyond any doubt. Peter explained that lives and worship were being transformed, just as the Old Testament had promised. In that time, the Spirit had fallen on special individuals for a particular task. But Israel's prophets had foretold a new age of the Spirit. The Spirit would no longer be just with the special few; he would be with all God's people. He would no longer inspire just for a special moment; he would live with, and even within, God's people for ever. Through signs and wonders, above all the sign of love and the wonder of God's presence, this new beginning would be quite unlike anything ever seen before. The dawn of the new age of the Spirit would be unmistakable.

Peter's message is simple – the promised new age has begun, and God has come down by his Spirit to live with his children. Peter's emphasis consistently concentrates on Jesus. Signs and wonders had marked Jesus out as the man of the Spirit, the promised Lord, and though he had been crucified, his life was set apart by God. Raised from the dead and exalted to heaven, he now pours out the Spirit on his followers. Peter's evangelistic invitation brings together his twin themes. His hearers must repent and be baptised in the name of Jesus. They also need to receive the promised Holy Spirit.

Only through Jesus's death and resurrection can the Spirit be given in this new way. Only through repentance and faith in Christ is the Spirit received. Life in the Spirit comes through the Giver of the Spirit. The focus of Peter's sermon is not his personal experience but the cross of Christ, because only the cross makes the new age of the Holy Spirit possible.

What went wrong?

The early Church knew they were the community of the Spirit. If the Spirit had been removed, most of what they were doing would have ground to a halt. If the Holy Spirit was removed from many churches today, would we as much as notice? Like Esau we have swapped our birthright for something trivial and passing. He was hungry, and exchanged his privileges as firstborn son for a bowl of gruel. We have traded in the glorious inheritance of the Age of the Spirit for a religion so insipid that the Church often seems to be a self-parody. The Church has exchanged the apostolic power that turned the Roman Empire upside down for socially respectable religious recreation, fulfilling for a few and irrelevant to many.

Two medieval churchmen watched gold-laden wagons coming into a church treasury, 'No longer,' one said smugly, 'does the Church have to say, "Silver and gold have we none."' The second replied, 'But no more can we say, "In the name of Christ, rise up and walk."'

Jesus promised that the Holy Spirit would come to unite and empower his disciples. We are the one vine, the one temple, the one family and the one body of Christ. But Christians have often either ignored the Spirit or used him as an excuse to separate from each other. A friend of mine was asked, 'Are you charismatic?' Since he was visiting a traditional Baptist church he had the sense to ask what they meant by 'charismatic'. 'A church-splitter,' was their categorical definition.

Polite company is meant not to discuss religion and politics. Polite Christian company has sometimes felt the same way about the Holy Spirit. The very words 'Holy Spirit' can be enough to encourage a stiffening of the spine or even kill conversation. A prickly, forced smile warns you to change the subject fast if you want to preserve the 'bond of peace'.

Some teaching on the Spirit is detailed on why everyone else is wrong, but doesn't have much positive to say. 'Balance' is a crucial word for understanding any biblical teaching, not just picking the verses you happen to like best. But 'balance' can all too often be made to mean 'Stay just the way you are.'

We all have horror stories about those we disagree with. Jim Packer tells a story of someone who knew two Pentecostal pastors who had left their wives. The man was most frustrated that Packer would not generalise from this vast statistical evidence that this sort of thing was bound to happen if ever you spoke in tongues!

We desperately need to get beyond such factional fighting and prejudice. Our strengths are often close to our weaknesses. Each of us in our worst light could furnish opponents with horror stories. What is more, the best distorted often produces the worst problems. As Shakespeare expressed it, 'Lilies that fester smell far worse than weeds.'

Rediscovery

I don't wish for one moment to give the impression that there are instant or easy answers. In a society of instant food, instant credit, instant everything, we crave an easy way out. That's escapism. But I do believe my Christian life had been painted into an unnecessary corner. The frustration and disillusion I felt weren't only the result of pride. They also grew out of incomplete teaching.

Jesus didn't promise the Spirit as an end to all our problems. But he does deliver us from the deadening staleness of a life without purpose. And he does take us beyond the discovery of our lack of inner power. When it seems that our failings will never let us go, we are not left on our own. But to put this into practice, we have to start rediscovering the Spirit. The Spirit is poured out for every Christian. We need more and more to reclaim the Holy Spirit for the whole Church. Above all, we need more and more to allow the Holy Spirit to reclaim each of us for the Father.

Many Christians recognise that the early Church was alive in the Spirit with a vitality hardly seen today, with a depth of love and power for evangelism. Their example drives us on to something more. The Church has been given the keys to the treasure house of the unsearchable riches of Christ, not just in theory, but in the living, experiential reality of knowing God's presence and love. Many Christians are hungry for clear, biblical teaching on the Spirit. Who is he? What is he like? What might he do to me? What about his gifts? Many want to discover a deeper fulfilment of the New Testament invitation and command to be filled, and continue being filled, with the Spirit.

Without the Spirit the Word can become dry. Without the Word, things apparently of the Spirit can become bizarre or even dangerous. But we don't have to choose one or the other. The two go together perfectly. As we explore Scripture in the power of the Spirit, together they can bring deepening maturity.

Evangelistic books are often invaluable for finding out more clearly what the Bible teaches, good reasons for Christian beliefs and what difference it all makes in practice. This book hopes to introduce the Spirit in the same way. Evangelistic books can help Christians know Jesus better. My hope is that you will know the Spirit better through reading this book. We will bring together biblical teaching and personal testimony to see the impact on everyday living of rediscovering the Spirit. We will examine the teaching honestly, to reach honest and practical conclusions. God is far more than theory and doctrine, just as love is more than words and talk. That means the Bible is a dangerous book to study. As we seek to rediscover all that the Bible promises about God's Spirit, we can expect him to be working to transform our lives.

2

Jesus and the Spirit

I shall always cherish the memory of children's cinema on Saturday
mornings, an experience I enjoyed in the sixties shortly before
television made it a practically extinct form of mass entertainment.
You could hardly hear the soundtrack for the noise. We screamed
and we cheered, we groaned and we booed. The building seemed
to echo with the munching of innumerable crisps. Someone was
always being firmly evicted by the scruff of the neck for kissing
the girls or puffing a furtive cigarette in the dark. The excitement
always mounted, whatever the distractions, for the programme was
getting nearer and nearer its climax – *Dick Barton, Special Agent*.
No matter how cruel the bad guys, no matter how fiendish their
plots, Dick would win through. No matter how deadly their traps,
just when it seemed impossible to survive, he escaped . . . but not
until the next episode. Two generations or more of British boys grew
up with the same dream: they would be like Dick Barton when they
grew up, or at least become like Snowy, his faithful assistant. Few of
our childhood heroes last. Dick must now be confined to libraries of
old black-and-white films. Most children apparently lose two other
idols between the ages of about five and eight. Mummy and Daddy
aren't perfect after all: they not only make mistakes, they can't even
always tell when you blame everything on your little brother!

Like it or not, we still have heroes in later years. I don't just
mean people we admire, but people we would love to be like.
Americans rather grandly call them 'role models'. There probably
arose a generation of British wives and mothers for whom Margaret
Thatcher became the dominant role model. Living rooms resounded

with a new phrase during domestic disputes over what wallpaper to choose or where to go on holiday: 'There is no alternative!'

As Christians, we too have our heroes. There are leaders and preachers we pay particular attention to, and churches we would like to be part of or wish our own churches to learn from. It may be someone like David Watson, who went to an almost empty church with the official task of closing it down. Instead he saw it transformed by the grace of God into a beacon of spiritual renewal, to which visitors came from all over the world. It may be someone like Jackie Pullinger or David Wilkerson, who proclaim the power of Christ to no-hopers, drug addicts and prostitutes, and see wretched lives healed. Or it may be someone like Corrie ten Boom, who learnt to forgive the Nazis who imprisoned her at Ravensbruck concentration camp, or Maximilian Kolbe, who substituted himself for a Jew under Nazi death sentence, and was executed in his place. We are surrounded by an ever-growing great cloud of witnesses (Heb. 12:1). It is good to have examples to follow, since they help us to see how to live as Christians in today's world. But we must watch out for hero-worship. Even the best of our heroes have feet of clay. Idols set up on pedestals are sure to bring disappointment in the end.

When it comes to the Holy Spirit, each of us needs to ask, 'Who are my role models?' Once again it is natural to have modern examples to follow. The curious thing is that we don't go straight to the obvious answer. We buff up the shine on our particular heroes, yet the answer of the New Testament is plain. Jesus is our ideal role model for what it means to be filled with the Holy Spirit.

The man of the Spirit

The fires of prophecy had not been rekindled for generations. Israel under Roman occupation continued to suffer the 'famine of hearing the Word of the Lord' that Amos had prophesied (Amos 8:11). God had entered a self-imposed silence but the hope for the coming Messiah had not expired. The presence of the Romans as yet another army of occupation intensified the ancient yearning for deliverance at the hand of God's Anointed Messiah. 'How long, O Lord?' remained the question on the lips of many faithful Jews.

With the baptism of Jesus, the Christian new age was inaugurated. John the Baptist had called the people back to God and to his holiness, describing himself as the forerunner, preparing the way for the Lord. As Jesus stood in the Jordan, the waters of baptism running through his beard, the promise of the prophets was fulfilled when the Holy Spirit, in the form of a dove, descended and remained upon him. The Spirit of the Lord had come to his chosen one and the age of the kingdom had dawned. As a result, Jesus could declare God's new beginning with consummate confidence: 'The time has come . . . The kingdom of God is near. Repent and believe the good news!' (Mark 1:15).

This spectacular anointing of the Spirit began Jesus's public ministry. His secret years of quiet preparation were over and he was now sent out with the message that would finally take him to Golgotha, the place of execution. However, before his public ministry could win followers and provoke enemies, the Holy Spirit first drove Jesus out into the wilderness – Luke uses a vigorous word of propulsion (Luke 4:1). Intense solitary prayer, combined with spiritual warfare, are shown to be necessary marks of God's new age. The voice from heaven had declared the unique role of the God-man, and almost immediately the voice of the tempter examined the true humanity of Jesus, for he was 'tempted in every way, just as we are' (Heb. 4:15). Withstanding every assault, Jesus's purity remained undefiled: he 'was without sin' (Heb. 4:15). This wilderness experience, in the power of the Spirit, prepared and strengthened Jesus for the three years ahead. Matthew and Mark both stress Jesus's authority in conflict with demons. Jesus possessed the power of the Spirit as no man ever had before.

Matthew adds some distinctive extras to the message of Mark. He is always concerned to stress Jesus's fulfilment of Old Testament prophecy. In the great moments of his life and in the tiniest detail, Jesus is always and unmistakably revealed as the Messiah. Between the temptations and the beginning of Jesus's preaching, Matthew inserts a prophecy from Isaiah: 'The people living in darkness have seen a great light; on those living in the land of the shadow of death a light has dawned' (Isa. 9:2; Matt. 4:16). In Jesus the promised hope has dawned. Anointed with the Spirit, Jesus radiates the holy presence of God upon the 'people living in darkness'. The Messiah has come.

Matthew stresses two more key insights, one at each end of his gospel. First, he provides some extra detail about Jesus's conception. Some people wanted to see Jesus as just another good man. For them, it was only when the Spirit descended at his baptism that Jesus became any different from the rest of us. At that point, because he had been so good, God decided to appoint him Messiah, and even adopt him as Son. Matthew will have none of that. The breath of God creates Jesus in the womb, but not as just another life. Jesus has no earthly father. Mary is 'with child through the Holy Spirit' (Matt. 1:19). This is stressed again in a similar phrase two verses later, by recording the words from Joseph's reassuring dream: 'the angel of the Lord ... said ... "what is conceived in her is from the Holy Spirit"' (Matt. 1:20–21).

John and Paul both go into greater detail when they explain the pre-existence of the Son of God. The Son has always been God, and there was never a time when he did not exist (John 1:1–2; Col. 1:15–17). He didn't suddenly arise at the moment of conception, but at this particular moment in human history, the divine Son took upon himself his human nature. Matthew's stress is equally emphatic on the continuing and unbroken presence of the Holy Spirit. The Spirit didn't come upon Jesus for the first time at his baptism. From the beginning of the incarnation, Jesus had continually been the unique man of the Spirit.

In the closing verses of his gospel, Matthew records the Great Commission: 'Therefore go and make disciples of all nations, baptising them in the name of the Father and of the Son and of the Holy Spirit, and teaching them to obey everything I have commanded you' (Matt. 28:19–20). John's baptism had been a baptism of repentance, turning away from the old life, but Christian baptism would be a baptism for believers who were entering into new life in Christ. The Spirit is set alongside the Father and the Son in the Great Commission in a remarkable departure from Jewish practice. All three are to be worshipped as the one God, and all three are involved in salvation. For Jesus and therefore for the gospel writers, the effective Church is inseparable from the Spirit, and the Spirit is indispensable for the task of mission (Matt. 28:18–20; Mark 16:15–20; Luke 24:48–9; John 20:21–2).

A glorious promise concludes the Great Commission, and with it Matthew ends his gospel. Jesus assures his disciples of his permanent presence with them: 'And surely I will be with you always, to the very end of the age' (Matt. 28:20). The promise needs no further explanation from Matthew. His first readers could move directly from the words of Jesus to their present experience of the Spirit. Jesus is with them, not just as an idea to write theology about, nor just as an example to follow. He is present in person. The man of the Spirit, through the gift of his Spirit, is experienced here and now as their living Lord.

Luke fills in more detail, as he confirms that Jesus brings about the new age of the Spirit. In his opening chapter, the birth of Jesus is heralded by the re-awakening of the gift of prophecy. The centuries-old silence of the Spirit in Israel is broken, for when Elizabeth and Zechariah prophesy they are full of the Holy Spirit (Luke 1:41, 67). Their experience follows the Old Testament pattern – their inspiration is only for that special moment. The coming of the Spirit upon Mary is linked directly to the incarnation of the Son (1:35). John the Baptist grows in the Spirit as a child (1:80). But while Jesus grows physically like any other child, he already enjoys the absolute fullness of the Spirit (2:40).

Immediately following his baptism, Luke emphasises the enduring, distinctive quality of Jesus's life. Jesus is 'full of the Holy Spirit' and is 'led by the Spirit in the desert' (Luke 4:1). Similarly, he returns from the temptations 'in the power of the Spirit' (4:14). When he reads in the synagogue at Nazareth, he claims to be not only a prophet (4:24), but the Anointed One, the definitive Servant of the Lord, upon whom the Spirit of the Lord has come, and in whom the ancient words of Isaiah are fulfilled (4:21). This public declaration at Nazareth was outrageous to Jesus's neighbours. How dare anyone make such a claim! This was the first time the authorities tried to kill Jesus. The fullness of the Spirit was already proving dangerous. In the next chapter Luke explains that in his healings as in his preaching, Jesus is the unique man of the Spirit (5:17). Luke's repeated emphasis upon the anointing of the Spirit in the early days of Jesus's public ministry is deliberate and unmistakable: at all times Jesus is empowered and filled with the Spirit. Through Jesus, filled with the Spirit, the wholeness, freedom and true deliverance of the Messianic age become possible. Only with Jesus is the presence and fullness of the Spirit made permanent.

The man of the Spirit demonstrates the permanent presence of the Spirit that the prophets had promised. The Spirit equips for public ministry, protects in temptation, empowers for teaching and healing, and guides in all things. In the Spirit, Jesus lived a life of love and prayer, with a remarkable freedom from normal human fears and anxieties. In his confident sense of the presence of God, the chasm is bridged between the transcendence of Almighty God and the ordinariness of daily human life. God can be with every single one of us in our everyday lives. Only through Jesus and only by the Spirit is this made possible. Jesus didn't offer super-supernaturalism – a life full of visions and no holidays. Nor did he offer respectable conformity – just like everyone else with extra religious trimmings. But he did show us what kind of life can be lived in the power of the Spirit.

The apostle Peter eloquently summed up the significance of the Spirit in Jesus's life when he preached to Cornelius: '. . . how God anointed Jesus of Nazareth with the Holy Spirit and power, and how he went around doing good and healing all who were under the power of the devil, because God was with him' (Acts 10:38). The first Christians were unanimous: life in the new age of the Spirit means living like Jesus. If you want to know what a Spirit-filled, Spirit-led life is like, look to Jesus. When you want a role model for spiritual living, don't look first to your modern heroes. Turn instead to Jesus, the man of the Spirit.

The giver of the Spirit

Some Christians think Luke's two books are like the family sagas that are often seen in television mini-series, where each episode tells the story of the next generation. It seems obvious that the first volume, Luke's gospel, tells us what Jesus said and did, and therefore the second takes us beyond Jesus to tell the story of the Spirit. Such a rigid distinction is a big mistake. For Luke, as for the other New Testament writers, the story remains the same. The Church belongs to Jesus and the Church's experience of the power of the Spirit is only possible through what Jesus has done. What is more, it is Jesus who now pours out the Spirit on his Church. With his resurrection and ascension, the man of the Spirit has also become the giver of the Spirit.

All four gospels establish this truth even before Jesus's public ministry begins. John the Baptist says he will be followed by the one who will 'baptise with the Spirit'. In fulfilment of the ancient prophecies, Jesus will have the authority to pour out the power of God. This close link between the Spirit and the risen Lord is found throughout the New Testament. For Paul, the Spirit can be referred to as 'the Spirit of the Lord' (2 Cor. 3:17), 'the Spirit of his Son' (Gal. 4:6), and even 'the Spirit of Jesus Christ' (Phil. 1:19). Peter also refers to 'the Spirit of Christ' (1 Pet. 1:11). The Spirit has been poured into our hearts (Rom. 5:5), and yet Paul can also refer to 'Christ in you, the hope of glory' (Col. 1:27). John similarly writes of the Spirit in our hearts as the sign of Christ living in us (1 John 4:13). Christ and the Spirit remain distinct, but the Spirit is the means by whom Christ is now with his Church. The Holy Spirit can by no means ever distract us from Jesus's historical death and resurrection, nor from Jesus's present authority as Lord of all. The power now at work within believers is the very power by which God raised Christ from the dead (Eph. 1:19–20).

This closeness of the Spirit and Jesus, and Jesus's role as giver of the Spirit, are spelt out at the end of Luke's gospel and the beginning of Acts. Jesus had taught that the Spirit would provide the disciples with the right words before rulers and authorities (Luke 12:11–12). In his last week in Jerusalem, Jesus adds that he will provide such words of wisdom himself (21:14–15). The role is the same, and Jesus will fulfil his own promise by means of the Spirit.

After his resurrection, Jesus promises that the disciples will be 'clothed with power from on high' (Luke 24:49). Then, just before the ascension, he recalls the prophecy of John the Baptist, and declares that their baptism with the Spirit is at hand – 'in a few days you will be baptised with the Holy Spirit' (Acts 1:5). Finally, he explains how these twin hopes fit together: 'you will receive power when the Holy Spirit comes on you' (Acts 1:8). Just as in John's gospel, it is Jesus who will send the Spirit. The Spirit is Jesus's parting gift to his disciples, the way the Church is brought to life, and the means of continuing Jesus's own ministry. Not until they receive the Spirit's power will the disciples become effective witnesses for Jesus.

We have already looked briefly at Peter's Pentecost sermon. He began with the disciples' spectacular new experience, but soon switched to Christ as his central theme. Again this conforms to Jesus's own teaching. While the event of their witness depends on the coming of the Spirit, the content of their witness is not primarily their personal experience of the Spirit or their new sense of joy and fulfilment. Though they are not afraid to describe these divine encounters, the gospel they proclaim centres on Christ crucified and raised. Christian witness should always be Christ-centred. Our chief concern is the historical sacrifice of atonement at the cross, provided and accomplished by our God of justice and mercy, for those who could not save themselves. Jesus summed this up in his resurrection appearance on the Emmaus Road: 'How foolish you are, and how slow of heart to believe all that the prophets have spoken! Did not the Christ have to suffer these things and then enter his glory?' (Luke 24:25–6).

At the climax of his sermon, Peter gets to the heart of this great truth. Jesus is not merely a good example. He was the unique man of the Spirit, 'accredited by God to you by miracles, wonders and signs' (Acts 2:22). More than that, he is now the giver of the Spirit. Only through Jesus, crucified and risen, is there forgiveness and new life, and only through Jesus can the Spirit be received. For it is this same Jesus, exalted as Lord, who pours out the Spirit on his Church. 'Exalted to the right hand of God, he has received from the Father the promised Holy Spirit and has poured out what you now see and hear' (2:33).

Some have suggested that Luke's second book would be best entitled the Acts of the Holy Spirit. Luke undoubtedly champions the vital presence and power of the Spirit: without the Spirit there could have been no Church, without the Spirit the apostles could not have begun their magnificent achievements. Others prefer the traditional title Acts of the Apostles, on the grounds that supernatural power required human heroism in obedience, action and self-sacrifice.

In actual fact Luke suggests a third possible title for his second volume. In the very first verse he refers back to his gospel. Volume One, he reminds the reader, covered the period up to Jesus's ascension. Then he uses an unexpected phrase. His gospel was not simply an account of what Jesus did and taught, but rather an account of what Jesus 'began to do and to teach' (Acts 1:1). Luke's confidence in both the personal experience of the Spirit and the objective Lordship of Christ leads him to a remarkable claim.

Through the power of the Spirit, Luke's second book records not merely the story of Jesus's followers but the continued actions and teachings of the Lord Christ. Luke's second book is the Acts of Jesus Christ, Volume Two, because Jesus is the giver of the Spirit.

The way the gospel writers present the Holy Spirit is distinctive and significant. Jesus taught that the supreme task of the Spirit is to glorify Christ (John 16:14), and the disciples followed his good example by sustaining a single-minded, glorious focus on Christ. Nothing could be allowed to distract, no matter how important, from Jesus as Lord. The gift of the Spirit came through the Son, and so the Spirit's presence could not possibly be seen as an alternative to Christ-centred Christianity. In Christ are found all the unsearchable riches of heaven. In Christ alone is complete salvation, deliverance from sin and adoption into God's new family. The coming of the Spirit is not in any sense supplementary to the work of the Son, as if grace in Christ was somehow incomplete and needed topping up. The availability of the Spirit is a part of Christ's glorious work of grace.

What is more, the Spirit doesn't just glorify the exalted Christ. He reveals and explains the historical life and mission of Jesus of Nazareth. The Spirit could continue to be known in present experience, but, just as Jesus had promised, he constantly prompted the Christians to recall and proclaim the words and works of Jesus: 'But the Counsellor, the Holy Spirit, whom the Father will send in my name, will teach you all things and will remind you of everything I have said to you' (John 14:26). The task of the gospels was to preserve and explore this central focus. Jesus's life and teaching, his incarnation, resurrection and coming again in glory were not merely incidental, they were absolutely crucial. Only in the person and work of Jesus could the reality and validity of the first Christians' encounters with the Spirit be explained. Only through coming to personal faith in Christ could others enter into the reality of new life in the Spirit.

In this chapter we have looked at Jesus and the Spirit. Jesus is the man of the Spirit: he is our true role model and shows us how to live in the Spirit. Jesus is also the giver of the Spirit: he pours out upon us the power that makes possible the Christian revolution of love. Some Christians talk as if they would prefer to do without the Spirit. They want to be 'Jesus only' believers. But the Jesus they claim to obey is the one who wants to enrich and empower us with the Holy Spirit. Others talk as if they can graduate from Jesus to the Spirit. But the Spirit is only available through Jesus and he delights in giving glory to Jesus. Neither extreme has a biblical leg to stand on. There is no justification in the New Testament for these ridiculous either/or attitudes – either Jesus or the Spirit. For the early Christians such thinking would be absolute and absurd nonsense. Quite simply, Jesus is giver of the Spirit, and Jesus and the Spirit go together perfectly. The biblical approach can be summed up like this: you can't have one without the other.

3

Jesus on the Spirit

I remember wondering as a child who on earth the ghost was that sometimes got a mention in prayers and hymns. I'm sure I wasn't the only one confused. Uncertainty about the Spirit has two results. First we become fearful of the Spirit, as if mentioning him might start up a kind of Christian seance. Too much talk about him threatens to turn a church building into a sort of Christian haunted house. Second, we replace him in the Trinity for all practical purposes with something more familiar. It has been said that some Roman Catholics worship Father, Son and the Holy Virgin; some Anglicans Father, Son and Holy Church; some Evangelicals Father, Son and Holy Bible; and some radicals Father, Son and Holy Revolution!

We like to think in pairs. Like love and marriage and the horse and carriage, the Father and Son fit together easily in our minds. We even divide the characteristics of the Godhead between these two, with a neatness which goes far beyond the Bible. Judgment pairs with grace, wrath pairs with love, and before we know it we have no room left in our thinking for a third party. The Bible speaks of the love of God and the wrath of God, never of the love of Jesus set against the wrath of the Father, but that's the way many Christians think in practice. Augustine tried to help us out of this corner of two-way thinking by suggesting that the Spirit is the bond of love who unites the other two.

Even the Apostles' Creed doesn't seem too sure what to say about the Spirit. The sections on the Father and the Son were developed partly to correct various heresies, but the compilers rightly included many clear and positive convictions. There seems to be an almost

embarrassed silence behind the single, unexplained statement of the
third section – 'I believe in the Holy Spirit'. We do indeed believe,
but surely more needs to be said than that?

Given this context, it really is no surprise that the most mysterious
member of the Trinity is often referred to as 'it'. 'It' is seen as cold
and impersonal, or even threatening and a little frightening. 'It'
can safely and wisely be left to the more emotional, or even the
over-emotional. Pentecost is so much more reassuring when referred
to as Whit Sunday. After all, the Spirit descended without warning
at Pentecost. If that was allowed today, whatever would happen to
the order of service? A friend of ours decided the mysterious 'it' was
not for her: 'Oh, I'm not interested in the Holy Spirit. "It" isn't my
scene at all!'

An all too common alternative to abandoning this mystery is to
recreate the Holy Spirit in our own image. If something strange is
going on, someone somewhere is bound to call it 'true spirituality'.
Some claim to have arrived. A higher plane of Christian living has
opened up before them. It is thrilling to hear all that God is doing.
But some talk as if the Holy Spirit shut up a small corner shop at the
end of the apostolic age, had a brief re-opening at the Reformation,
and has now flung open the doors of a fully refurbished spiritual
hypermarket.

My wife, Claire, once heard an enthusiastic speaker explain that
Spirit-filled Christians don't need holidays. The Spirit simply keeps
them going. No biblical evidence was given for this astonishing
claim, which came as a relief to me. I rather enjoy holidays, and
it had seemed for a moment that my low-level spirituality had been
once-for-all exposed! Neither avoiding the Spirit, nor unbiblical
fantasy will do. When it comes to finding out what the Spirit is
really like, we need to turn to the Bible. In this chapter we will
look at what Jesus taught about the Holy Spirit.

God's best gift

Jesus wanted to assure his disciples that the gift of the Spirit can be
welcomed with open arms, and so he presented God as the supremely
loving Father. Presumably as many children endlessly demanded
things from their fathers then as do now. Perhaps it's because

Dad is seen as a soft touch, but holiday resorts and supermarkets often echo with the same request: 'Daddy, please may I have just one more?'

Jesus shows how perverse it would be to betray a child's simple trust by suggesting that each request of the child might be met with the wrong gift. What is more, each faulty gift is at best useless, and at worst positively dangerous. A request for bread earns a stone, a fish wins a serpent and an egg gains a scorpion. The humorous exaggeration and caricature are typical of Jesus. Then Jesus adds a double twist. No decent human father would consistently betray good requests with dangerous gifts (Luke 11:11-12), and this is so even when human fathers are 'evil', that is, sinful (11:13). But if human fathers know how to give good gifts, how much more dependable is the incomparable goodness of the heavenly Father.

Matthew takes the story as far as the general principle of God the Father's absolute reliability – 'How much more will your Father in heaven give good gifts to those who ask him!' (Matt. 7:11). Luke emphasises Jesus's specific and decisive punchline about the Holy Spirit. Both are agreed that Jesus encouraged prayer for good things and promised that such prayer would be answered. Both are agreed that God's gifts are gifts of grace, given through his love, and not because we deserve rewards. But Luke recognises that Jesus taught that the Holy Spirit is the best gift of all, the supreme expression of God's fatherly generosity. Jesus's teaching confirms that it is right to ask the Father for more of the Spirit. In fact Jesus positively encourages such prayers. He also seeks to neutralise any fears about receiving the Holy Spirit. Jesus provides all the reassurance he possibly can that God's best gift is very good indeed: 'how much more will your Father in heaven give the Holy Spirit to those who ask him' (Luke 11:13).

Born of the Spirit

With Nicodemus, Jesus discussed the nature of salvation, revealing that each person's eternal destiny is not based on religious pedigree or social respectability, but on spiritual rebirth (John 3:1–21). Jesus describes rebirth in two ways, one of which is very familiar – we need to be *born again* (3:3). Though more developed in the passage,

Jesus's second phrase is less used among Christians today – we need to be *born of the Spirit* (3:5–8).

In Greek as in Hebrew, the word for Spirit can also mean 'breath' or 'wind' – *pneuma* in Greek, *ruach* in Hebrew – and when Jesus speaks of the wind of the Spirit he is drawing on a rich strand of Old Testament teaching. In creation, God's Spirit hovered over the waters to bring forth order, beauty and life (Gen. 1:2). When Adam was created, God breathed into his nostrils the breath of life (Gen. 2:7). This may simply mean that, having fashioned a human bodily form out of the dust, God then gave the miracle of life to Adam. More likely it speaks of Adam's discontinuity with the rest of the creatures of the earth, being endowed as a spiritual being with a distinctive capacity for relationship with God. In Isaiah, the sovereign breath of God that gives life can also blow to bring death – 'he blows on them and they wither, and a whirlwind sweeps them away like chaff' (Isa. 40:24). In Ezekiel, the wind of God is instrumental in God's work of regeneration. In prophecies that look forward to the work of Christ, God declares that he will take away our hearts of stone and put within us a new Spirit, that will bring about a change of heart and life (Ezek. 36:26–7). He will put his Spirit within people and they will live (Ezek. 37:14). Ezekiel's prophecies about being reborn of the Spirit are dramatically focussed upon his vision of the valley filled with dry bones (37:1–14). Ezekiel's first prophecy is to the bones, but that achieves only a partial success. Although they come together, they remain lifeless – 'there was no breath in them' (37:8). Then he receives a second command, this time to prophesy to the breath – 'Come from the four winds, O breath, and breathe into these slain' (37:9). Have you ever wondered whether it is biblical to use such prayers as 'Come, Holy Spirit'? Well here is conclusive evidence and a solid biblical precedent. When the Spirit came, the dry bones could live again, even as Jesus taught that we need to be born of the Spirit.

In his discussion with Nicodemus, Jesus not only emphasised new spiritual birth, but also took up the theme of the Spirit's continuing unpredictability (John 3:8). The wind blows where it wills, and no one can tell where it comes from or where it is going. Even so, when the wind of the Spirit blows upon a life, a new dynamic and dimension are imparted. There is an old story of the Church being like an office building with all the windows fastened shut and many papers stored neatly in piles. Someone opens the windows, and the workers enjoy the breeze of fresh air. But very soon the papers start to get blown about. Dismayed at this disruption of orderliness and control, the leaders close the windows once again. All too often the Church has been tempted to prefer tidy, human religion to the fresh and unpredictable breezes of the Spirit. A becalmed yacht is a sorry sight, but it's always thrilling to see the raised sails swell anew when once more they catch the wind. The task of believers is not to control, let alone ignore the wind, but rather to live out new surprises from God, as we respond to the breath of his Spirit.

The personal Spirit

In Jesus's last week in Jerusalem he spoke about the Spirit more than ever before. This is found in great detail in John 14–16. Throughout John's gospel, Jesus refers to God as 'the Father' and as 'the one who sent me'. In the teaching of this last week parallel phrases are now used about the Spirit:

> I will ask the Father, and he will give you another Counsellor
> . . . (John 14:16)
> . . . the Holy Spirit, whom the Father will send in my name
> . . . (John 14:26)
> When the Counsellor comes, whom I will send to you from
> the Father, the Spirit of truth who goes out from the Father
> . . . (John 15:26)
> Unless I go away, the Counsellor will not come to you; but
> if I go, I will send him to you. (John 16:7)

John confirms time and again that Jesus is the Giver of the Spirit, and that the Spirit's coming is only possible through the death of Jesus. What is more, the Spirit is sent at the request of Jesus, and comes, like Jesus, from the Father. This represents some of the most profound thinking about the Trinity in the New Testament. Jesus and the Father are one. All that belongs to Jesus belongs to the Father. And the Spirit will not act independently, but will make known all that belongs to Jesus, just as Jesus has only acted according to the will of the Father. The activities of the three are distinct and yet indivisibly one.

We could easily overlook in translation John's deliberate and emphatic underlining of Jesus's message. By the use of many impersonal metaphors for the Spirit – the oil, fire, wind and rain of God – the Old Testament leaves open the possibility of referring to the Spirit as 'it'. John reveals that Jesus denied this categorically for all who follow him. John could have referred to the Spirit as 'it'. In fact, according to Greek grammar he should have. Just as 'table' in French is feminine – *la table* or *elle* – in Greek 'spirit' is neuter – *to pneuma*. When John mentions 'the Spirit', he uses the correct neuter form of 'the'. But where grammar requires him to say 'it', John deliberately wrote 'he'. You can imagine the shock for his first readers. It would have been as unmistakable as when an Englishman in France shouts '*le table*' or '*il*'. (The English always assume that foreigners are a little deaf.) The nearest equivalent in English would be to write in capital letters: HE.

This is no accident on John's part. He deliberately writes bad grammar to emphasise good theology. He wants above all to be faithful to the teaching of Jesus. And so John stresses it as strongly as he can, *the Holy Spirit is not 'it', but 'HE'*. The Spirit is not a sanctifying spectre about which we cannot be too sure. He retains all his Old Testament qualities, but the Holy Spirit is a person. He is as personal as Jesus, and he is as much and as fully God as are the Son and the Father. Any dilution of this emphasis is less than Jesus taught. Anything less fails to capture the first principle of Jesus's teaching on the promised Spirit: 'Unless I go away, the Counsellor will not come to you; but if I go, I will send HIM to you' (John 16:7).

What is the Spirit like?

The Spirit may be personal, and even God, but what is God like? Faced with the infinite God, the most profound human thinkers are soon out of their depth. To the psalmist, such knowledge is beyond his reach – 'it is too high' (Ps. 139:6). Isaiah stressed the irreducible chasm between human finitude and divine transcendence – our thoughts are not his thoughts, nor our ways his ways (Isa. 55:8).

Men before God are no greater than grasshoppers – our behaviour is as insignificant as an insect's scurrying (40:22). Even the great nations are like dust on the scales (40:15).

This leaves us with an enormous problem. God reveals himself through his actions, through the Bible and through his people. We are bound to want to talk about him. The need to describe him is part of the need to know him. But where do we begin? One solution is to play the big word game. The more syllables in a word, the more profound it can seem. Soon a collection appears – omnipresent, omniscient, omnipotent. Someone even wrote a hymn about the consubstantial, co-eternal Trinity. These words have their place, but they soon leave most of us with verbal indigestion. God is personal. That's why Jesus taught in parables and not in complex abstractions. That doesn't mean abstractions are useless, but they are not very good at communicating a living relationship.

Philip the apostle shared our problem. Jesus had spoken vividly and often about the Father, but Philip still found it somehow remote and theoretical, and so he made his plea: 'Lord, show us the Father and that will be enough for us' (John 14:8). Jesus's reply is revolutionary. He didn't reflect on the otherness of God in his absolute transcendence of human categories. Nor was there a supernatural visitation in the room of the manifest presence of God. Rather, Jesus revealed himself to be the supreme revelation of the character and will of God. Jesus spoke so categorically that it would have been blasphemy on anyone else's lips, because he claimed an absolute correlation between his own character and the Father's. He didn't suggest modestly that he was a pale and partial reflection of God, but rather claimed to be the definitive self-revelation of God in human flesh: 'Anyone who has seen me has seen the Father' (14:9). This is the very heart of the gospel. If you want to know what God is like, look to Jesus. If you want to know God's response to human sinfulness and rebellion, look to Jesus. If you want to see God reconciling the world to himself, look to Jesus. For in Christ Jesus, 'all the fullness of the Deity lives in bodily form' (Col. 2:9).

There is only a small step from Jesus's revelation of the Father to our present theme. The Spirit is personal and has the same origin as Jesus. The Spirit reveals Jesus and is sent by him. Therefore, if we want to know what the Spirit is like, we need above all to look at

Jesus, as he is portrayed in the four gospels. This close identification of the Spirit with Jesus can provide us with much reassurance. It takes us right away from super-supernaturalism that wants to leave Jesus behind and pass to higher things. There is no higher revelation than Jesus Christ, and Jesus not only promised the Spirit, he also shows us what, or rather who, the Spirit is like. Just as Jesus reveals God the Father, he also reveals the Holy Spirit.

Another Counsellor

Some friends of ours were legal guardians to another couple's children. That couple were tragically killed while abroad. Our friends could never replace the children's real parents. But they stood in their place. Nothing could make up for the terrible loss, but the children knew they would never be abandoned. Their foster parents would do everything for them that they possibly could. The disciples were faced with a similarly devastating loss. For three years they had been led and taught by Jesus. They had given up their jobs to travel where he travelled. Now they had arrived in Jerusalem, and the sense of adventure was upon them. Following the triumphal entry of King Jesus, things were bound to come to a head. They listened to Jesus with bated breath, and all their hopes were dashed. The Romans would stay in Israel. Jewish religion would not be reformed. The Master had come to the City of God not to reign on earth, but to die.

When the disciples were utterly dismayed, Jesus gave his fullest explanation of what the Holy Spirit is like. Jesus promised the disciples that they would never be left on their own. His departure would mean the coming of *another Counsellor* (John 14:16). There are two words in Greek that mean 'another'. John could have chosen to use the word that means 'another of a different kind' (*heteros*). The Greek word he actually uses (*allos*) has a distinct stress – the new Counsellor will be another of the same kind. The new Counsellor will be another *just like Jesus*. In fact, so faithfully will the Spirit reveal and glorify Jesus that he may be described as the presence of Jesus in Jesus's absence.

John's Greek word for counsellor, 'paraclete', is particularly rich in meaning. The Authorised Version used the word 'comforter' with the intention of conveying what is now the long-lost emphasis of bringing the strength needed for action (*con fort*, with strength). This old meaning of comforter was brought home to me vividly a few years ago when we visited the Bayeux Tapestry, a wonder of the early medieval period that celebrates the triumph of William the Conqueror in 1066. When the decisive battle is raging, and the outcome is not yet clear, William's half-brother, Odo de Conteville, the Bishop of Bayeux, is shown 'comforting' the Norman soldiers (panel 54). The word on the tapestry is '*confor*', and the official French and English translations both use the word 'encourage'. What is significant is the means of comfort, for rather than the bishop gently soothing his battle-weary troops, Odo is seen brandishing a mighty wooden club above their heads. His 'comfort' is to spur the Normans on to renewed acts of valour. When the Holy Spirit 'comforts' the troops of Jesus, he is not simply 'gentle, meek and mild', for there is a battle to be fought and a world to be won!

Jim Packer cast a wide net round the meaning of 'paraclete' with the following list: comforter, strengthener, counsellor, helper, supporter, adviser, advocate, ally, senior friend (J. I. Packer, *Keep in Step with the Spirit*, IVP, 1984). The Spirit comes alongside the disciples of Jesus to continue Jesus's own ministry. His particular help will reflect our particular need. Lesslie Newbigin provided a complementary net of meanings: the Spirit calls, beseeches, entreats, comforts, consoles, exhorts. He adds that these words sum up the very stuff of the Christian life together – 'no human achievement but as a gift from the Father' (Lesslie Newbigin, *The Light Has Come*, Handsel Press, 1982). The only other New Testament use of 'paraclete' is in 1 John 2:1. There the paraclete is Jesus, who 'speaks in our defence' before the Father. This confirms the protective role of the Spirit. He is the best defender of the faith, both within our hearts and before the world. He is 'another comforter' even as Jesus is the first comforter.

The promise of Jesus goes far beyond providing a substitute for himself, or an equivalent to a legal guardian. As Christ has been for three years to his disciples, even so will the Spirit be in the future. He will be the presence of Jesus for them and for all Christians, not just for three years, but to the end of the present age. Each year after the crucifixion would seem to take the first believers further from Jesus. The death of each apostle would seem to take the early Christians still further away from him. And each generation that followed would appear to be condemned to having a still less certain grasp on the Saviour. Not so, Jesus explained! Because the Spirit is 'another Jesus', as the Spirit illumines Scripture and inspires our hearts, Jesus is ever present with us. The quite astonishing promise is that the presence of Jesus will never fade away. That doesn't mean we don't need the gospels: they have been given as the authoritative record of Jesus's life and teaching for every generation. But in every generation, informed by those gospels, the presence of Jesus will remain just as real.

If we want to know what God is like, we look to Jesus. If we want to understand the ministry of the Spirit, we look to Jesus. Nowhere is Jesus seen more clearly as the Counsellor than in the last week before his crucifixion. The quiet, reassuring confidence of his words brought peace to his disciples then, and has spoken afresh to every generation of disciples since: 'Do not let your hearts be troubled. Trust in God; trust also in me' (John 14:1). The mystery of the Spirit can make us fearful. We either run fast from him, or we remake him in the image of our own experiences. Jesus shows us a better way by explaining and demonstrating his person and ministry to his disciples. In the Holy Spirit, Jesus comes to us. He neither gift-wraps our faults nor manhandles our frailties, but by pointing us to the love of the Father, just as Jesus did for the disciples, the Holy Spirit meets our deepest needs.

Intimate presence

Many people instinctively think of God as 'up there' and 'out there'. He 'reigns on high', and that can often seem immeasurably far from our everyday world. Prayer can become like a very long-distance telephone call with a poor line. We talk about prayers 'hitting the ceiling'. It's as if the prayers that 'get through' pass beyond the roof and through the atmosphere, finally reaching God at some remote distance. This way of thinking also tends to confine God to special places. We begin to feel God is only present in religious buildings – the houses of God. Then it helps if they have an old-fashioned, medieval feel about them. When Liverpool Cathedral was built in traditional Gothic style, one national newspaper commented that

God prefers Gothic. A friend of ours belongs to a church whose building is very modern. When outsiders come to view it, in case they want to be married there, some have been heard to say: 'It's really not suitable at all. We want to get married in a proper church!'

Jesus's teaching about the Spirit is very different from this 'up there' and 'out there' way of thinking. His promise of the Spirit's presence broke new ground in four decisive ways. First, the Spirit comes forever (John 14:16). We no longer receive temporary inspiration, which was the most that could be expected for the Old Testament prophets and heroes. We don't even enjoy a special intervention by God for a limited period, like the three-year ministry of Jesus. Instead, for every generation and in every part of the world, Jesus promised the permanent presence of God's Spirit.

Second, the Spirit comes to be with us personally (John 14:17). The Spirit doesn't live in buildings made of bricks and mortar. He cannot be trapped or contained in church buildings, or locked up safely with the church silver. The gift of the Spirit isn't for Sundays and special religious occasions only. He is God with us.

Third, the Spirit will be within us (John 14:17). This may sound familiar. Many Christians are used to the concept of the 'indwelling' of the Spirit. But the longest journey truth has to make is the journey from head to heart. The breakthrough comes when we make it practical and personal. God lives in ME. Put as bluntly as this it sounds almost blasphemous, if Jesus had not been the first to say it. It can help a great deal to stop three times each day for a week simply to pray: 'Thank you, God. It really is true. Your Spirit lives in me.'

Fourth, we can be at home with God (John 14:23). Some years ago, when we had recently moved to Bromley, there was a knock at the front door. I opened it, and to my surprise I was faced with a policewoman, who asked if she could come in for a few minutes. My mind raced as I invited her into the lounge. Had I been speeding or had I driven through a red light? Could I have committed some major offence without knowing it? I felt thoroughly guilty, but tried not to act as if caught red-handed. Every step to the lounge was one more step of the sentenced prisoner towards the condemned cell. As we sat down, I braced myself to hear that anything I said might be taken down and used in evidence against me. After what seemed an eternity, the clouds cleared. She was a friend of the people who used to own the house, and simply wanted their new address. One thing was certain. Until I found out why she was there, I was certainly not at home, even though Claire and I were the ones paying the mortgage. I think the policewoman rather enjoyed my few moments of innocent discomfort!

Home is where you relax. You feel accepted for who you are. There's nothing to prove to anyone, and you don't have to be constantly on your best behaviour. You can be yourself, and put your feet up. You soon know if you're not at home with someone. Conversation becomes difficult. You begin to perch awkwardly on the edge of a chair. It can be your own house, but some people make you feel no longer at home.

Jesus makes his promise about the permanent presence of the Spirit as plain as possible – 'If anyone loves me, he will obey my teaching. My Father will love him, and *we will come to him and make our home with him*' (John 14:23). Christians can give up those old ideas about a far-away God, 'up there' and 'out there'. He doesn't 'come down to be with us' only when we meet for worship. Not only is the Holy Spirit right here with us and within us at all times, but the living God even wants to make his home with us.

Jesus could not possibly say this lightly. It does not diminish the awe-inspiring holiness, majesty and power of God, nor does it domesticate God, reducing him to the status of a pagan household god. What it does describe is the possibility of an extraordinary intimacy with the Living God. Because there is no condemnation for those born again in Christ (Rom. 8:1), and because the Spirit is within us and encourages us to know God as 'Abba, Father' (Rom. 8:15), we really can be 'at home' with God. In the new age of the Spirit, God comes down to make his home with us, at all times, in our own houses, in our daily routine, and wherever we go. Jesus's own life demonstrates this sustained intimacy in action. As we learn to live by the Spirit, we can reclaim our glorious inheritance in Christ and rediscover what it means to be at home with God.

The Convictor

The Spirit who brings us the wondrous love of God is also the Spirit of holiness. Jesus teaches that while the Spirit's presence is

a source of great hope and joy for believers, for the world the
impact of the Spirit is rather less pleasant, for he comes to convict
of sin (John 16:8–11). Jesus describes a threefold conviction, of sin,
righteousness and judgment. If we are to come to saving faith we
need to understand that we fall short of God's requirements; we
must recognise that without Christ we lack positive righteousness;
and we must face the reality that this world is in thrall to the prince
of darkness, who despite his apparent triumphs has already been
defeated at the cross.

Our society is more comfortable with the concept of guilt feelings,
subjective reactions that require counselling if they get out of hand.
This is because our society would like to reject the idea of moral
absolutes, preferring a DIY, pick-and-mix approach to morality, in
which everyone creates their own personal code of conduct and does
what is right in their own eyes. What Jesus describes is real, objective
guilt, that needs real, objective atonement and forgiveness. That's
because Jesus teaches that there are indeed moral absolutes, summed
up in the Ten Commandments, by which every single person will be
judged by God.

In Jesus's teaching, conviction of sin is a preliminary work of
the Spirit, a preparation for his indwelling of a new believer. The
convicting work naturally continues in every Christian, but now he
unmasks our sins in an environment of mercy and grace. We do
not lose our salvation every time we sin again, for we have been
born again of the Spirit and into Christ, once for all. If we water
down the reality and severity of the judgment of God, we impede
this convicting work of the Spirit. We have to grasp the sinfulness
of sin and the reality of judgment if we are ever to grasp the enormity
of Christ's self-sacrifice and the totality of the salvation that he has
won for everyone who believes. For some in every generation this
has involved a profound and even protracted agony of conviction
before they come through to saving faith in Christ.

There is a crucial distinction to be made between conviction and
condemnation, for unbelievers and Christians alike. The Holy Spirit
convicts of sin to bring home our need of the Saviour. Spirit-inspired
conviction of sin leads to repentance and forgiveness. Satan is
content to condemn us in our sin, seeking to crush us with
unremitting despair at the deficiencies in our character. When
the Holy Spirit points out our sin, his work is regenerative. He

consistently points us to the cross of Christ where our guilt is transformed into hope, and every stain of sin is washed away.

Spirit of truth

We conclude this examination of what Jesus had to say about the Holy Spirit with a phrase to which Jesus returns repeatedly in John 14–16. The Holy Spirit is the Spirit of truth (John 14:17; 15:26; 16:13). The context for this teaching is found near the beginning of chapter 14, when Jesus describes himself as 'the way, the truth and the life' (14:6). Jesus makes a claim for himself that is beyond all human convictions and opinions, all philosophies and religious ideas. He presents himself as nothing less than the self-revelation of God in human form. Not a human means of reaching after God, but the divine means of rescuing humankind. In short, Jesus stakes an explicit claim to being the provider of absolute truth – 'No-one comes to the Father except through me' (14:6). The Spirit who is sent by Jesus is therefore the first defender of the truth of Jesus.

The Spirit of truth is the Spirit of doctrine. He reveals both the intimacy within the Godhead between the Father and the Son, and also the security of the believer who is enfolded by the firm grip of the love of Christ (John 14:20). The Holy Spirit who brings us encounters with divine love also stirs us to love God with all our mind. To put this in personal terms, the same Spirit meets me in worship, preaching and prayer in our church and as I travel around; he meets me when I am walking our dog in the beauty of Wimbledon Common; and he also meets me in my study, helping me to think rigorously about the Christian faith.

The Spirit of truth also loves to teach, for Jesus promises that he will teach us 'all things' (John 14:26). Jesus doesn't imply that the Spirit is a fount of useless information: he is a teacher not of trivia but of all things necessary for the faith. Specifically, Jesus explains that his disciples will be reminded by the Spirit after Jesus's ascension of everything he has said. This is a threefold promise: first to the gospel writers – the Spirit will inspire their books; second to those taken before the courts – the Spirit will inspire their defence when they are persecuted for Christ's sake; third to all believers in every generation – the Spirit loves to enrich our understanding of Jesus.

The Spirit of truth is not locked up in a university library, for he also delights to witness to Jesus (John 15:26). There is great encouragement and inspiration for our efforts at evangelism in the simple observation that, in the book of Acts, wherever the Christians travel to witness to Jesus, the Holy Spirit not only accompanies them but he has been there first. When Philip meets the Ethiopian eunuch, he has been studying Isaiah 53 and is eager to hear more about the Suffering Servant (Acts 8:26–38). When Peter gets to Cornelius' house, the entire household is ready to be saved (Acts 10). In every century of church history, the Holy Spirit has been the first and finest witness to Jesus.

Finally, the Spirit of truth is the Spirit of revelation. He will not only help us recollect what Jesus said and did, he will also guide us into all truth (John 16:13–15). Jesus spells out three aspects of this continued revelatory role: the Spirit will only speak what he hears, bringing truth from the Father and the Son; the Spirit will speak into the future of the Church and the world, between Jesus's ascension and return; and the Spirit will always speak in ways that glorify the Son (to 'glorify' the Son means to be cross-centred as well as Christ-centred, for in John's gospel the glorification of Jesus is rooted emphatically in the cross – e.g. 7:39; 17:1). What this means is that the Spirit continues to be at work in the history of the Church, in preaching and prophecy and also in doctrinal deliberations. The rediscovery of the doctrine of justification by faith at the time of the Reformation does not simply demonstrate the theological expertise and acumen of Luther and Calvin, but is a classic example of this continued revelatory work of the Spirit. Since the Spirit is always at work, we have much to learn from church history and tradition. The wise evangelical will reject both extreme positions: either of despising church history as irrelevant and old-fashioned or reverencing church tradition as infallible. The Spirit of truth who has guided past generations will enable us both to learn from our forebears and to evaluate their contribution critically by the unchanging yardstick of the Scriptures.

This revelatory dimension of the Spirit of truth operates not merely in past generations, but also in the present day, and his methods need to shape our thinking. The Holy Spirit will never contradict the Scriptures that he inspired, and nor should we if we want to know his help and favour. The Holy Spirit seeks the glory of Christ rather than seeking centre stage himself, and we must ensure that we are consistently Christ-centred in personal ministry and church life, neither switching the focus to the Spirit nor to ourselves. The Spirit of truth is the Spirit of servanthood: he guides us into all necessary truth, not for his own interest but for our benefit and for the glory of Christ.

We began with the apparent mystery of an impersonal Spirit, but Jesus's gloriously rich teaching conveys the unmistakable promise that encountering the Spirit doesn't mean experiencing some vague impersonal force. The Spirit who continues the ministry of Jesus is like Jesus. He is God's best gift to those who are born again. He is personal and like Jesus. He comes to us as another Counsellor and brings us intimacy with God. He is the Spirit of holiness who convicts of sin, and the Spirit of truth, in doctrine and teaching, in witness and continuing revelation. The glorious confidence of the New Testament is this: to live by the Holy Spirit is nothing less than to experience the presence of Christ.

4

Popular excuses for avoiding the Spirit

Politicians are masters of excuses. If we don't like their policies, they talk about the cure that needs a bitter pill or the feel-good factor that is yet to work through the system. If that fails to distract us, they will decry the failures and excesses of the opposition, and insist there is no real alternative. Ask them a straight question, and they'll try anything rather than give a straight answer.

In evangelism we become familiar with popular excuses. Often they are knee-jerk responses that attempt to avoid any hard thinking about Jesus himself. Many people think they are being very original in their objections to the Christian faith, when really we have heard the same excuses many times before. Jesus was just a good man; you can't change human nature; you can't believe in God these days; and so on. Once we have recognised the most common excuses, we can arm ourselves with relevant and informed responses. It's rare for a well-prepared Christian to be caught off guard by a completely unexpected objection to faith.

Nietzsche hit on one very popular excuse for avoiding Jesus: 'His disciples will have to look more saved, if I am going to believe in their Saviour.' Faced with such frankness, we have to acknowledge the failure of Christians to live up to their calling, both in previous generations and today. But the experienced Christian witness need never be thrown by such tactics. Nietzsche was pointing in one direction, that is at the Church, in order to avoid someone else, namely Jesus Christ. When we meet this familiar excuse we seek to defuse it by bringing the objector face to face with Jesus in the gospels. No one has ever taught like Jesus. No one has ever lived like Jesus. His claims about himself and the way he actually lived make a perfect fit. He is indeed the way, the truth and the life.

It's hardly surprising that people turn to popular excuses for avoiding Jesus Christ: if what he taught is true, the implications for the way we live are revolutionary. What may come as more of a surprise is the fact that born-again believers often use popular excuses to avoid the Spirit of Jesus. They use slogans to try to dodge his impact on their lives, and to try to convince themselves that there is nothing more to discover or receive. Many Christians have attempted this kind of evasive action. Time and again we are faced with the same, familiar excuses. We shall turn to popular excuses for avoiding the spiritual gifts in a later chapter, but we now turn to popular excuses for avoiding the Holy Spirit and the need to be filled.

Excuse one: I got it all at conversion

This is an excuse that can bristle with defensiveness. When some hear talk of being filled with the Holy Spirit, they react in this way because such words seem to bring into question the reality of their conversion. Only by the Spirit can anyone confess that Jesus is Lord (1 Cor. 12:3). Only by the Spirit can anyone confess that Jesus is truly God's only Son (1 John 4:15). Only by the Spirit are we grafted into the body of Christ in the first place (1 Cor. 12:13). If anyone does not have the Spirit, then he does not belong to Christ (Rom. 8:9). The New Testament witness is unanimous: whoever receives Christ as Lord and Saviour also receives his Spirit. The complete absence of the Spirit could only mean no conversion, being still separated from Christ and not yet incorporated into his body.

In the early Church, new converts were given a thorough grounding in teaching about the Holy Spirit, in theory and in practice. They didn't just receive him on the quiet, subconsciously without even noticing it. They entered without fear or apology into the fullness of life in the Spirit. By great contrast, our problem is not that we didn't receive the Spirit at all, but rather that in many churches, no one ever told us anything about him, except perhaps some horror stories to illustrate the excesses to avoid. It's as if an elderly aunt put a large sum into a bank account in your name but neglected to pass on the good news, with the result that you fail to enjoy the benefits of the rich inheritance that is already yours. For many Christians, our first problem is ignorance: the gospel we were originally taught is substandard and incomplete.

We need to recover a clear conviction that every Christian receives the Spirit at new birth but that this is not the same as being filled with the Spirit. Every believer needs to be filled and refilled with the Holy Spirit, and such fillings are not designed to be so subtle that we might not even notice they have occurred. The first Christians were filled with the Holy Spirit and they knew it, quite unmistakably. Any lack of evidence of the work of the Spirit in those first believers was never passed over in embarrassed silence or explained away with superficially reassuring words about not relying upon subjective experiences. On the contrary, the absence of the Spirit's presence in power required an urgent diagnosis and decisive action. When Philip was faced with a distinct lack of evidence that the Samaritan converts had been filled with the Holy Spirit, he sent to Jerusalem for a team of apostolic troubleshooters to come and sort things out (Acts 8:14–17). Luke records that when Peter and John placed their hands upon them, they at last entered into a definite experience of God's presence: 'They received the Holy Spirit' (8:17). When Paul discovered that the Ephesians who introduced themselves as disciples actually knew nothing of the Holy Spirit, he immediately suspected they had not yet been born again. Paul led them to Christ, baptised them as new believers, and then laid his hands upon them in prayer. As a result, 'the Holy Spirit came on them, and they spoke in tongues and prophesied' (Acts 19:6). To receive the Spirit in unmistakable power was the normal Christian experience in the early Church.

'I've got it already' can easily serve as the cover for disbelief ('There's nothing more for me to receive'), or even for rejecting the Spirit of God ('I've got all that I want or need'). Where this happens, the biblical truth that every believer receives the Holy Spirit at conversion becomes distorted into a popular excuse. What this excuse tends to mean in practice is not simply 'I've received some already,' but a much more arrogant assertion: 'I've got it all.' Such an attitude has all the hallmarks of spiritual pride or complacency. Unless we can truly say that we are clothed with power from on high and walking in perfect holiness, there is not the slightest credibility to such a claim. To Martyn Lloyd-Jones this feeble excuse for avoiding the Spirit was completely unacceptable: 'If you have got it all, why are you so unlike the New Testament Christians? Got it all? Got it all at your conversion? Well, where is it I ask?' (*Westminster Record*, September 1964).

I have never met a Christian who has got it all, and every single one of us who hasn't 'got it all' needs to go on being filled with the Holy Spirit.

Excuse two: Talk about the Holy Spirit distracts from Jesus

A child with a brand new toy can talk of nothing else. Infatuated young lovers have eyes only for one another. In the same way, some Christians are so thrilled to discover the Holy Spirit that they seem unable to talk about anyone else. Meanwhile, other Christians hardly ever mention the Holy Spirit, believing that they bring honour to the Son of God through a 'Jesus only' brand of Christianity. Neither of these extremes is found in the New Testament. Only through the cross of Jesus is the Spirit given, and so it is only thanks to Jesus that we can receive the Spirit of God at all (John 7:39). It is the Spirit who equips the Church, but we become part of the body of Christ, not the body of the Spirit (1 Cor. 12:12–13). The Spirit's constant delight is to bring glory to Jesus (John 16:14).

Claire and I used to live in York, where the land is fairly flat and the city planners, to their great credit, have restricted the height of new buildings to preserve the medieval skyline as much as possible. Over the city towers York Minster, one of the most beautiful Gothic cathedrals in Europe. At night the Minster is floodlit, and the warm yellow stonework has a glorious and unforgettable glow. You can see the Minster clearly from far beyond York's ancient city walls. The building is so vast that from a distance it seems almost to hover above the city. The vision of the medieval craftsmen has been preserved and even enhanced. As if set on a hill, the majesty of God is eloquently declared by the Minster's breathtaking grandeur, even at night.

Modern floodlights are nothing like the sweeping searchlights used in the second world war. They are discreetly concealed and precisely directed. They neither draw attention to themselves nor bathe in light the night sky or the buildings surrounding their 'target'. Those in York glorify the Minster superbly, while never distracting attention to themselves. This is how the Spirit relates to Jesus. He has a divine floodlight ministry. He lights up the glory of the Son.

In his evangelistic preaching, Paul constantly returned to the theme of Christ crucified, not using rhetorical tricks, but with 'a demonstration of the Spirit's power' (1 Cor. 2:4). Only the Spirit can floodlight the message of the cross, turning it from something that appears to be nothing more than 'foolishness' into 'the power of God' (1 Cor. 1:18). Even so, confession of faith is only possible through the Spirit, and so Paul explains that it is only by the Holy Spirit that Jesus can be confessed as Lord (1 Cor. 12:3). Similarly, John provides a test of the Holy Spirit that is centred on Jesus: 'This is how you can recognise the Spirit of God: Every spirit that acknowledges that Jesus Christ has come in the flesh is from God, but every spirit that does not acknowledge Jesus is not from God. This is the spirit of the antichrist . . .' (1 John 4:2–3). By the ministry of the Spirit men and women are pointed to Jesus as Lord, both in conversion and in our continuing declarations of living faith.

The fullest exploration of this floodlight ministry is provided by Jesus himself. When Jesus promised the Spirit, he directly connected the coming of the Spirit with the new realisation that 'I am in my Father and you are in me' (John 14:20). Jesus's divinity and every Christian's new status in him are both revealed by the Holy Spirit. The Spirit never does his own thing, but he 'speaks what he hears' from Jesus (John 16:13). This never-ending Jesus-centredness (that is, Christocentricity) of the Spirit that leaves neither place nor purpose to blowing his own trumpet reaches its fullest expression in John 16:14: 'He will bring glory to me.' As the floodlights bathe York Minster every evening, the Holy Spirit delights to shine upon Jesus's glory.

Although the Holy Spirit always points beyond himself, this should not be taken to mean that Christ is best glorified by never mentioning the Spirit. He is the Spirit of Jesus, sent from the Father and the Son. When we talk about the Spirit biblically, it is Jesus who is glorified. As Jesus prepared his disciples for his imminent crucifixion he didn't talk about the Holy Spirit to the exclusion of all else. But, as we saw in chapter 3, the promised coming of the Spirit was a central theme to Jesus's teaching during his final week in Jerusalem when he laid the foundations for the future Church (John 14–16). Jesus and the apostles recognised that detailed and direct teaching about the Spirit is absolutely vital.

You cannot pick and choose between Jesus and the Spirit. Talking exclusively about the Spirit would inevitably distract from Christ, but glorifying Christ is no excuse for avoiding the Spirit. If we pass over the Spirit in cautious whispers or an awkward silence, we play down the One whom Jesus has provided for us, and such an attitude is appallingly dishonouring not only to the Spirit but also to the Son. The more we are open to the Holy Spirit, the more useful to Jesus we will be. That's why Jesus insisted that his followers should not get started on the task of the Great Commission until they had been 'clothed with power from on high' (Luke 24:49). Genuine openness to the Spirit will always cause us to bring glory to Jesus Christ.

Excuse three: It's all emotions

When Peter and John healed the man at the Beautiful Gate, the result was quite a stir in the temple. After all those terrible and degrading years of paralysis and begging, his legs had been made whole at last. He didn't just walk into the temple to thank God, he skipped and leaped his way around those hallowed precincts, and quite literally jumped for joy (Acts 3:1–10). It's reasonable to assume that some of the temple priests were not at all pleased. You can imagine their snide criticism: 'That's what happens if you mix with the followers of Jesus – you lose all sense of respect for the house of God!' There's no suggestion that the healed paralytic praised God by leaping about for the rest of his life. Perhaps he never again actually jumped for joy in the temple. But his heart surely must have leaped within him whenever he remembered all that Jesus had done for him that day.

Middle-class British people find it notoriously difficult to express emotions. When we are so far out of touch with our own feelings, any emotional display in public is likely to make us uncomfortable. We are quick to label almost anything as over-emotional, especially where God is involved. A letter to *The Times* a few years ago recognised the illogicality of this peculiar prejudice:

Why is it that if a cinema comedy produces laughter, the film is regarded as successful; if a theatre tragedy brings tears to the eyes of the audience the production is regarded as touching; if a football match thrills the spectators, the game is reviewed as exciting; but if the congregation are moved by the glory of God in worship, the audience is accused of emotionalism?

I remember hearing two very different sermons on emotions. An Anglican vicar warned his respectable parishioners about the dangers of excessive emotion, where the gospel is reduced to mere froth and bubbles, and to getting a good feeling. A Pentecostal pastor cautioned his flock about the desert of a mind-dominated, emotion-free Christianity, where new life in Christ can wither away into no more than a dry-as-dust theory. Both were right, but how I wish they had been preaching from one another's pulpits. As it was, each reinforced the instinctive prejudices of their own congregation. We see other people's over-emphasis so much more clearly than our own!

The word normally used for 'worship' in the New Testament (*proskuneo*) literally means 'I come towards to kiss.' That's the kind of intimacy we need to rediscover in worship. Courting couples don't often discuss at great depth the psychology of interpersonal behaviour. They usually find more value in saying over and again those time-honoured words: 'I love you.' There is always a need for thoughtful hymns of worship, expressing in great poetry all that we have been given in Christ. But there is also room for simple love songs to express the intimate and overflowing love of sinners before their Saviour. The bride of Christ needs to take time to declare from the heart, 'Jesus, we love you.'

Fear of emotions can make us very emotional, with the result that we run scared from a healthy wholeness in worship. Some traditional Western Christians would find the worship of ancient Israel completely unbearable and over the top. All kinds of horrors have been read into styles of worship that the ancient Israelites would have considered perfectly normal. There were celebratory psalms that got really excited about their national deliverance from Egypt; meditative psalms considering the glories of God's law; enthusiastic psalms that praised God with very simple words and a great deal of repetition. Some psalms allowed God's people to tell him just how terrible they felt, and even to complain that they felt so hard done by. This type of psalm seems to have been linked to temple prophecy: you could get your bad feelings off your chest, but then you had to wait, humbly and expectantly, for God's response through the prophet.

The accompaniment to the psalms was as varied as the words. Many different kinds of stringed instruments were played, along with pipes, drums and cymbals. Psalm 150 clearly required a substantial Hebrew orchestra:

> Praise him with the sounding of the trumpet,
>> praise him with the harp and lyre,
> Praise him with tambourine and dancing,
>> praise him with the strings and flute,
> praise him with the clash of cymbals,
>> praise him with resounding cymbals.
> Let everything that has breath praise the LORD. (Ps. 150:3–6)

Then there was the festal shout. At special celebrations the cry went up from the people: 'The Lord reigns!' This great shout of praise and triumph would make the temple and the city ring. In fact the Old Testament contains nearly as many invitations to shout for joy as to sing for joy. Some people ask why modern worship has to be so noisy. But if we use the yardstick of the worship of ancient Israel we have to ask a different question: where has all the shouting gone?

As well as many instruments and much singing and shouting, there was a great deal of movement. Some psalms describe a dramatic procession of singers, marching through the temple or even around the city. They clapped their hands, stood in God's presence, raised their hands and also prostrated themselves before him. What is more, their worship included dancing. You may have noticed it in Psalm 150, mentioned just after the tambourines, which the dancers probably held to accompany themselves. Singers and dancers alike would join in praising God, the source of their vitality (Ps. 87:7). There were even times when the whole of the congregation may have been invited to express their worship in spontaneous dance:

Let Israel rejoice in their Maker;
> let the people of Zion be glad in their King.
Let them praise his name with dancing
> and make music to him with tambourine and harp. (Ps.
> 149:2–3)

Jeremiah delighted in this glorious Jewish experience of worshipping God with our bodies as well as our voices. When he prophesied the new covenant, he foretold that in the coming age there would be abundant joy. What is more, in the worship of the new covenant he prophesied that dances of joy would find a special place:

They will come and shout for joy on the heights of Zion;
> they will rejoice in the bounty of the LORD . . .
Then maidens will dance and be glad,
> young men and old as well.
I will turn their mourning into gladness;
> I will give them comfort and joy instead of sorrow.
> (Jer. 31:12–13)

Because God made us, all that we are, our bodies and emotions as well as our minds and voices can be put to good use in worship and in our walk with God. Jesus wept in public before Lazarus' tomb, and our emotions too are given for appropriate expression, not to be hidden away guiltily, far from public view. Paul told us to learn to weep with those who weep, and rejoice with those who rejoice. He didn't expect us to repress all our feelings so that we never rock the respectable boat of formal Sunday religion. In everyday life we are constantly using non-verbal communication in the way we sit and move. Many use gestures to reinforce what they say. Many Italians are so good at it that I have followed a complete conversation without understanding more than a handful of the spoken words. There really is no biblical reason why anyone should ever be expected to sing the praise of the living God while standing stiffly to attention!

Many British Christians are like pressure cookers, locking away their pent-up emotions deep within. They desperately need the pressure to be released, and rediscovering emotions in worship takes the lid off the pressure cooker. Of course, some can become so captivated by emotions that for a while they go completely over the top. Emotions are one part of us to be expressed in worship, but emotions are not the focus or purpose of worship. True worship is very likely to lift your feelings. But if you look to feelings instead of to Jesus, living worship will begin to shrivel. Before long, your emotions will become dry and bland, stale and worn out.

The Holy Spirit never gives us emotion for emotion's sake. But we need to remember Jeremiah's prophecy that the new covenant will bring exuberant rejoicing. Luke's phrase for the immediate impact of the divine presence captures the same kind of emotional response – 'filled with joy' (Acts 2:28; 8:8; 13:52; 14:17; 16:34). When I first became a Christian I was given the impression that Christian joy was a rational conclusion that completed by-passed the emotions. Christ has died and I have put my trust in him. Therefore I am joyful, QED. Each week I heard the congregation make the same request, 'And let your chosen people be joyful.' But so far as I could see it made no difference to anyone. Christians have sometimes turned miserableness into the prince of virtues. Sometimes whole churches behave like a cartoon character who is walking around under a perpetual cloud of rain – wherever he goes, rain is sure to fall. Such is the complete absence of joy in some churches that they behave less like the bride than the widow of Christ. This is not the normal Christian life that the apostle Peter commended. His description of fullness of joy is one of the most graphic sentences of the New Testament: 'Though you have not seen him, you love him; and even though you do not see him now, you believe in him and are filled with an inexpressible and glorious joy' (1 Pet. 1:8).

There is nothing more exciting to discover than the incredible truths of the cross of Christ and the immensity of the love that God is willing and eager to pour out upon his people. When the Spirit brings home to us the glories of our salvation, an emotional response is both natural and inevitable. While we certainly want nothing whatsoever to do with hype or emotional manipulation, the main problem with the Christian Church in Britain is not that we have an excess of emotion but rather that our hearts have grown so cold. When the Spirit of God has been poured out upon me, I have both *felt* and *thought* with an intensity I have never known in any other experience of life. The conventional Christian allergy to emotion is not a virtue but a vice, and the sooner we are cured of it the better.

Excuse four: It's all triumphalism

Triumphalism means disguising the cost of discipleship as a never-failing success story. It means glamorising the gospel as a fail-safe way to an easy life. Triumphalism isn't based on service of God. It is rooted in self-fulfilment, with a familiar question: 'What's in it for me?' Triumphalism parades the spiritual equivalent of advertising slogans and plays down the cost of living for Christ and the demanding realities of everyday living.

The Philippians were probably Paul's favourite church. They had a lot going for them, and didn't suffer from the turmoil and confusion Paul had to try to sort out in some church plants. Then some difficulties arose. The other citizens of Philippi began to oppose the Christians (Phil. 1:28). Cracks opened up in the fellowship. Some grabbed status for themselves. Some concentrated only on their own clique. Others settled into a routine of constant complaints and arguments. Their question for Paul was plain: 'Why is Christ the conqueror letting us be treated like this?'

Paul wrote to them from prison. He had previously been imprisoned in Philippi itself, and had been miraculously freed by the Holy Spirit (Acts 16). But this time there had been no sudden deliverance. The Spirit has not guaranteed to provide that particular solution to every experience of persecution. God's interests were now best served by Paul being taken to Rome, the very heart of the Empire, under military escort. If we want to recover the great triumphs known by the early Church in the power of the Spirit, we also have to be prepared to follow them in the way of the cross. The Spirit of Jesus is the Spirit of supernatural rescues, but he is also the Spirit of the martyrs.

Paul wanted the Philippians to rejoice despite the facts of his imprisonment and their own persecution. The Spirit doesn't keep us clear from every difficulty, but he does help us to praise God in spite of them. More than that, Paul's hope was that the Philippians might come to see their suffering as a privilege, and not just a problem: 'For it has been granted you on behalf of Christ not only to believe on him, but also to suffer for him' (Phil. 1:29). This is not said lightly. No one should ever presume to say such a thing casually or unthinkingly to someone who is suffering. But Paul writes with credibility and authority because at that very moment he is himself suffering for Christ, probably to a greater degree than any of the Philippians.

Life in the Spirit doesn't mean brushing our problems under the carpet and pretending they don't exist. The Spirit helps us to accept the hard times, to trust that God will use them for good, and to rejoice in Christ, even when it hurts. Of course that's not always easy, but it's the way of reality and maturity if we want to grow in the Spirit! True spiritual maturity is in a completely different league from the specious claims and artificial glamour of the fantasy world of triumphalism. If someone tells you that the Holy Spirit guarantees a lifetime of success and prosperity, their understanding of the lives of Jesus and Stephen, Peter and Paul, Hosea and Jeremiah is pathetically deficient. Paul's highest aspiration was not a problem-free existence, but 'to know Christ and the power of his resurrection and the fellowship of sharing in his sufferings' (Phil. 3:10).

Excuse five: I'm too afraid of the Spirit to receive

Fear of the supernatural is a very natural reaction. Faced with a power that is awesome, beyond the power of human control, we are bound to feel out of our depth. That is surely why the Bible reports that the first words of angelic visitors are usually something like 'Fear not', or 'Don't be afraid.' In the same way, Jesus frequently had to allay the fears of his followers in his resurrection appearances.

> The angel said to her, 'Do not be afraid, Mary . . .' (Luke 1:30)
> The angel said to them, 'Do not be afraid.' (Luke 2:10)
> Jesus came and stood among them and said, 'Peace be with you!' (John 20:19)
> Though the doors were locked, Jesus came and stood among them and said, 'Peace be with you!' (John 20:26)

A number of fears cluster around our instinctive reactions to the Holy Spirit. First, there is misunderstanding about the Spirit and his work.

The old name 'Holy Ghost' had a tremendously unhelpful impact on the imaginations of many generations. A ghost is a mysterious apparition which may not exist at all but frequently provokes considerable fear and disquiet. The 'Holy Ghost' therefore sounds decidedly spooky, either a fanciful illusion produced by fevered imaginations or a spectral presence left behind by Jesus. Sound biblical teaching on what the Holy Spirit is like is the best cure for this particular kind of fear.

Others are afraid of a particular impact of the Spirit of God. I remember praying for one man who was clearly thirsty to receive more, and yet it felt as if we were praying for someone wearing a suit of armour. Every defence was up and he seemed to be concentrating intently upon resisting our prayers. We stopped praying and asked what was going on. He confessed that he was so scared of falling over that he was putting every effort into making sure that it didn't happen. Not everyone falls over when they are filled with the Spirit, nor in my experience is any other reaction universal. Some weep, some are filled with joy, some shake, some speak in tongues, some show rapid eye movements or fluttering eyelids, some become dreamy, some become filled with new vigour. What Jesus asks of us is that we come to him to be filled, with no strings attached. It really doesn't help to pray, 'Lord I surrender my life to you afresh today. Please fill me with your Spirit, and do what you want in my life. But I definitely don't want any of the following manifestations or spiritual gifts!' That young man had to concentrate on what really mattered – his need to be filled – and leave it to Jesus to sort out the immediate reactions and the long-term consequences.

Some have a non-specific fear of anything that doesn't usually happen in their particular church. We need to remind these cautiously conservative believers that the Church was born in the unusual. The resurrection was entirely without precedent in the history of the human race, and the resultant outpouring of the Spirit at Pentecost resulted in experiences of God, new languages of worship and an empowered evangelistic preaching unlike anything ever seen before among the Jews. Since the Church was born in surprises, the Lord of the Church reserves the right to do the unusual in every generation. The real surprise is not that the Holy Spirit does the unexpected, but rather that the Church has so often settled for the predictable and unchanging, the regimented and the safe. We have grown accustomed to a pale and insipid imitation of the dynamism of the first Christians, who were unmistakably clothed with power from on high.

Others fear losing control. Their whole life is built around a professional detachment. They want to do the right thing and remain composed in all circumstances. They embody the stiff-upper-lip virtues of Kipling's advice to prospective leaders in the British Empire:

> If you can keep your head when all about you
>   Are losing theirs . . .
> If neither foes nor loving friends can hurt you,
>   If all men count with you, but none too much;
>   . . . you'll be a Man, my son!

Such people are the walking wounded. Some have been emotionally deprived as children, and have coped with the traumas of parental rejection or the loneliness of a boarding school by building impregnable defences around their longing to be loved. Others have been trained in patterns of Christian discipleship or leadership that leave no place for personal vulnerability. I remember one minister who asked for prayer with the confession that he was doubly paralysed: by fear of others' reactions to him and by the need to be always in control in his relationship with God. As we prayed for him tears slowly rolled down his cheeks, then he fell to the ground and began to shake. I turned to a member of the prayer ministry team and commented, 'I don't know what the Lord is doing, but I think something is definitely happening to this man's excessive self-consciousness!' Later he wrote to me saying that the glory of the Lord had laid him low. On the floor he experienced overwhelming revelations of the love of Jesus, combined with a profound sense of spiritual surgery on his inner being as the Spirit removed his heart of stone and gave him a heart of flesh. He also experienced the physical sensation of an intense supernatural heat that burned all over his body. The next morning he was amazed to see that the part of the floor where he had been lying had lost its shine; the living flames of love that had burned healing into his inner being had melted the floor polish clean away!

Another common problem is the fear of failure: 'What if they pray for me and nothing happens?' Sometimes this arises from previous disappointments that haven't been followed up wisely. For others the origin is low self-esteem: they find it so much easier to believe that God will bless others than that the Holy Spirit would ever have time for them. Such people are tempted to rush away quickly after a moment of prayer, or may even interrupt those praying for them after a single sentence, writing off the ministry with an abrupt and premature conclusion: 'There you are, I told you nothing would happen to me!' We need to ensure that they are genuinely seeking God and not pinning all their hopes on a particular manifestation or gift, but more commonly they are almost overwhelmed by negative expectations even before they make their request for prayer. Such people need gentle reassurance that they are truly and personally loved by God. Avoiding every possibility of manipulation or pressure they need to be helped to take time with God, not merely to acknowledge him but, as Hosea expressed it, to 'press on to acknowledge him' (Hos. 6:3). As they persist with God in an environment of care and support, they will in time break through into liberating encounters with love from on high.

Jesus not only reassured his disciples with words spoken directly against the power of fear, he also sought to overcome our natural fears in his description of fatherly kindness. Just as normal human fathers are reliable, and their children trust them implicitly to provide good things, Jesus personally guaranteed to us the supreme reliability of our Father in heaven: 'If you then, though you are evil, know how to give good gifts to your children, how much more will your Father in heaven give the Holy Spirit to them who ask him!' (Luke 11:13).

For some people, fear is dealt with by meditating upon the promises and reassurances of the Bible. Others need to take time before God, acknowledging their hang-ups and asking Jesus to take them beyond their fears. I sometimes tell people they need time to defrost in God's presence, not rushing away but quietly standing or sitting before God, allowing supernatural love to melt away their fears. One young man came forward for prayer who knew he needed more of God and yet was almost literally petrified. He stood so stiffly he was practically rigid as he confessed his fear. I reassured him that this was a perfectly normal reaction, and that far from condemning him, Jesus understood his fears and wanted to help him leave them behind. I explained that I wanted to pray that God would gradually defrost him, melting the fears away. If he wanted further prayer before the meeting came to an end, he could ask for it, but there was no obligation to go any further. After all, if he was freed from the grip of fear, that would be a major step forward in itself. When I prayed for him, he began to weep quietly before God, as he trusted Jesus with the mountainous enormity of his terrors. It was like the laser machine in the film *Honey, I Shrunk the Kids*, as Jesus reduced his fears into an ever smaller compass. The Everests of his anxiety shrank to mere molehills, until at last he felt safe to entrust his life fully into the hands of God and be filled with the Holy Spirit. His request for prayer had begun with the confession that he had never felt so terrified, but when God melted away his fears he was able to declare with a radiant face that he had never felt so wonderful, because Jesus had filled him with supernatural love and glorious joy.

Reasons or excuses?

Most of the objections we have looked at have some value in correcting an unhealthy, unbiblical overstatement. But reasons often turn into excuses. We hide behind other people's mistakes to try to avoid the Spirit. That means quenching the Spirit within us and shutting out any deeper experience of his presence. The popular excuses for avoiding the Spirit won't wash. They are a cover-up for the fact that we want to keep control of our own lives. We prefer to keep a firm grip on how much real influence we will hand over to God.

Jesus didn't call us to have one hundred and one reasons why our particular church has got everything right. He called us to follow him. If I have the most carefully worked out theology of the Spirit, and use it to avoid being filled, my theology is worthless. It has become an evasion, a barricade for my sinfulness, for my self-sufficiency or for my fear. It has become, quite frankly, no more than another evasive excuse. The message of the New Testament is plain. Give up your favourite excuses for avoiding the Spirit. Know the Spirit's presence, with you and within you. And go on, day by day, being filled afresh with the life-giving, life-transforming Spirit of the living God.

5

Be filled with the Spirit

Standing waist deep in the River Jordan, John the Baptist called hundreds, maybe thousands, to repentance, but he was clear about his own limitations and spelt out the difference between himself and Jesus. While he could baptise with water, only Jesus had the divine authority to baptise with the Holy Spirit. John called people to repentance, but he knew that the ultimate transformation of our lives, nothing less than the decisive liberation from our sinful nature, required something more: a transcendent gift from God himself.

In the Old Testament it had never been suggested that God's presence was an experience for experience's sake. There is always a moral force to moments of divine inspiration. God's holy power came down upon a few for the benefit of many. Military leaders were inspired for victory in battle, ensuring the future of Israel. Kings were anointed for right ruling as God's special representatives. Prophets were inspired to demand moral goodness in private, commercial, and political dealings. When Yahweh breathed out his Spirit, leaders and spokesmen for true holiness stepped from anonymity into the public eye. Their new authority was unmistakable. Despite the many key leaders the Spirit inspired, however, his coming throughout the Old Testament period was always restricted. He only inspired special people for special events at special times. John the Baptist's words therefore declared something very different – Jesus would bring a new and universal baptism with the Spirit.

The Old Testament prophets had foretold this breakthrough to a new age of renewal and holiness. A future king, uniquely anointed with the Spirit, would bring this about, for the Spirit of the Lord would be upon him to declare and bring God's favour to his people (Isa. 61:1–3). In this coming age of the new covenant, God's moral power would make inner change possible, as God wrote his law on human hearts (Jer. 31:33). Jeremiah even hints that the ancient Israelite priesthood will be rendered obsolete, as a result of a new and universal intimacy with God (31:34). Ezekiel declares the promise that a new heart of flesh will replace our hearts of stone (Ezek. 36:26) as God puts his Spirit within his people. In both Jeremiah and Ezekiel the same meaning is clear: by his Spirit, God will begin changing people on the inside in a remarkable and revolutionary way. The Breath of God who is the source of life will make possible the renewal of life. There will be no preferential treatment for kings, priests or prophets, for the Spirit will come upon all believers. Joel, whose prophecy was quoted by Peter at Pentecost, when the Spirit first came in this new way, spelt out the inclusiveness of this promised outpouring. Young and old, women and men, everyone would be able to know the impact of the Holy Spirit upon their lives.

> I will pour out my Spirit on all people.
> Your sons and daughters will prophesy,
>> your old men will dream dreams,
>> your young men will see visions.
> Even on my servants, both men and women,
>> I will pour out my Spirit in those days. (Joel 2:28–29)

Spirit baptism

The Greek word *baptizo* helps us to understand how much of the Holy Spirit John expected us to receive from Jesus. It was not a technical or religious term, but was rather a familiar word from everyday life. If someone had drunk a glass or two of wine, this word was an inappropriate description. Only if they had drunk one or two bottles could they be said to have been baptised with wine. If an inexpert oarsman was struggling to master his craft, splashing water into the boat with every stroke, even though his incompetence might make him more than a little damp, his boat could not be said to be baptised. But if a boat was caught in a terrible storm, the wind whipping up waves that crashed over the bows and storm clouds delivering a torrential downpour, such a boat, so filled with water that it was close to capsizing, could justifiably be described as baptised with water. In short, baptism speaks not of a light sprinkling but rather of a dipping, immersing or drenching.

When Claire and I visited the Niagara Falls, the spray began to catch our faces many metres away from the closest viewing points. Only when we were in the tunnels behind the falls, seeing and hearing the awesome force of tens of thousands of gallons of water crashing past our eyes every second, could we begin to grasp the magnitude of this natural wonder. Some ten years ago a young boy fell into the river above the falls. The current tore him from the arms of rescuers and in moments he was swept over the brink. Survival seemed an impossible dream. Beneath the falls, someone on a tour boat was amazed to see a little body bobbing in the waves and he was fished out, battered and breathless, yet somehow still alive. Now that was a boy baptised in Niagara!

Since Jesus's intention is to baptise us with the Holy Spirit, his desire is not merely to deposit an occasional drop of the Holy Spirit upon us, whether at conversion, believers' baptism or confirmation or at any other time, but rather to drench every believer in the life of God. This total immersion was certainly what happened on the day of Pentecost, when the first believers were overwhelmed by God's presence. They were indeed immersed in the Holy Spirit, 'filled to the measure of all the fullness of God' (Eph. 3:19).

So what exactly is Spirit baptism and when does it take place? The English word 'baptism' has taken on a religious meaning that is more complex than the Greek term from which it is derived. On the one hand it speaks of initiation. This is hardly surprising, since water baptism is almost universally understood as a rite of initiation, whether of infants or new believers. At the same time baptism retains the older meaning of immersion. This is applied literally to water baptism among those who immerse those being baptised, but the implication of the abundance of God's presence in Spirit baptism is retained among those whose use of water is more restrained.

Those who emphasise that 'baptism' speaks of initiation rightly observe that every believer is 'born of the Spirit', has received the Spirit, and confesses that Jesus is Lord by the Spirit. Therefore, they argue, every Christian has been baptised with the Spirit. Those who emphasise that 'baptism' speaks of immersion argue that there is a need for our experience to correspond with that of the first Christians. It is not enough to assert that every Christian has received the Spirit. Jesus explicitly connected the first Christians' Spirit baptism with their experience of being 'clothed with power from on high' (Luke 24:49). The danger for the first group is that they neglect to emphasise the need to be immersed in the Holy Spirit. As a result they may be tempted to disparage other Christians' more dramatic spiritual experiences. The danger for the second group is that they may discount the preliminary reception of the Spirit. As a result they may be tempted to corner the market in the Holy Spirit, and suggest that other Christians know nothing of him at all.

In fact, both are partly right. The Spirit is indeed given to every believer at conversion, and every believer is meant to be immersed in the same Spirit. For the first Christians, there were four foundations to Christian initiation: repentance from sin; saving faith in Christ; water baptism; and finally Spirit baptism. While the order may vary, all four aspects are integral to a complete Christian initiation, what some have called a normal Christian birth. Baptism with the Spirit is begun when the Spirit is first received, but is not complete until the believer has been immersed in the Spirit of God. What is more, baptism with the Spirit does not mean that one immersion is sufficient for life. After our initial Spirit baptism, the normal Christian life will require many more fillings.

Every filling with the Spirit in the New Testament was a definite experience of God's presence. In Acts 2 there were audible and visual signs – the sound of wind and tongues of fire (Acts 2:2–3). They spoke with tongues, declaring the wonders of God (2:4,11), and Peter preached under the Spirit's anointing with such power that three thousand were converted and baptised. It was clearly apparent to unbelievers that something unusual was happening, but while some expressed an intrigued amazement, others merely mocked, saying that the believers must have drunk too much. In Acts 4 the same believers were filled again. This time the room shook and they 'spoke the word of God boldly', which may be a description of emboldened witness or a new release of prophetic words (4:31). This second filling demonstrates three important principles. First, it is not only possible but advisable to be filled with the Spirit more

than once. Those who had been filled previously didn't opt out of
receiving on this occasion, as if they had already had their fair and
full share of the Spirit. Second, we should note that these first two
fillings were both corporate. While Luke also records instances of
individuals being filled on their own, on most occasions several
people, and often whole gatherings of believers, are filled with the
Spirit together. Third, it's not enough to say that while we are open
to the Spirit in terms of the slow process of inner sanctification, that
is growth in holiness, we are not comfortable with the thought or
possibility, let alone the necessity, of actual experiences of being
filled with the Spirit. The Spirit's work is about both process and
crisis. It is certainly true that he wants to shape us gradually into
Christ's likeness throughout this life, but being filled with the
Spirit can never be marginalised as a matter of personal taste
and temperament. Luke consistently emphasises, in church after
church and individual after individual, that the Spirit comes upon
us in sudden and dramatic ways, when he fills us with heavenly
love and clothes us with divine power.

Luke records eight occasions when people are filled with the
Holy Spirit (the Jerusalem church twice, the Samaritans, the
Ethiopian eunuch, Saul, Cornelius' household, the Philippian
jailer's household and the Ephesians – Acts 2, 4, 8 (twice), 9,
10, 16, 19). The event itself is described by Luke in several ways:
being baptised with the Spirit (Acts 1:5), filled with the Spirit (2:4;
4:31; 9:17; 16:34), the Spirit coming on them (8:16; 10:44; 19:6) and
receiving the Spirit (8:15, 17). Three times hands are laid on people,
three times the gift of tongues is mentioned, twice people are filled
with joy, three times they speak the Word boldly and once they
prophesy. In short, there is no one method of praying or sign of
being filled that is always present and immediately apparent. The
evidence of the New Testament simply does not justify the assertion
that baptism with the Spirit must always be accompanied by tongues,
nor by any other spiritual gift or emotional or physical reaction. The
Spirit comes upon us as the sovereign Lord and declines to always
work in exactly the same way. It's quite mistaken to say that if you
haven't received one specific gift you cannot possibly have been
filled with the Spirit.

However, while we cannot insist on one particular sign of the
Spirit coming upon people, in every event that Luke records there

Filled with the Spirit

— what happens during the eight visitations recorded in Acts

	'Filled with the Spirit'	'The Spirit came on them'	'Received the Spirit'	Hands laid on	Tongues	Prophecy	Speaking the word boldly	Joy	Several filled together
Jerusalem Acts 2	✓	✗	✗	✗	✓	(✓)[1]	✓	(✓)[2]	✓
Jerusalem Acts 4	✓	✗	✗	✗	✓	(✓)[3]	✓	✗	✓
Samaria Acts 8	✗	✗	✓	✓	✗	✗	✓	✗	✓
Ethiopian Acts 8	✗	✓	✗	✗	✗	✗	✗	✗	✗
Saul Acts 9	✓	✗	✗	✓	(✓)[4]	(✓)[4]	✓	✗	✗
Cornelius Acts 10	✗	✓	✓	✗	✓	✗	✗	✗	✓
Philippian Acts 16	✓	✗	✗	✗	✗	✗	✗	✓	✓
Ephesians Acts 19	✗	✓	✗	✓	✓	✓	✗	✗	✓

NOTES

[1] By implication, Peter's quotation from Joel suggests there was prophecy, although Luke does not mention it directly.

[2] Since they were declaring the wonders of God (2:11), we can assume there was an overflow of joy.

[3] Luke's phrase, 'speaking the word boldly' might speak of witnessing or prophetic words or both.

[4] We know that Paul spoke in tongues and prophesied (1 Cor 14:6,18), but we don't know when he first received these gifts.

was invariably some unmistakable evidence of a power encounter with the presence of God. Every filling in Acts is a memorable, crisis experience in the presence of God. When there was no experiential evidence that the Samaritan believers had received the Spirit, they weren't advised to play down experience and simply believe. On the contrary, Peter and John made an emergency apostolic visit and laid hands upon them, praying for the Spirit to come upon them. I vividly recall my confirmation as a teenager, when the presiding bishop laid hands upon me, declared over me, 'Receive the Holy Spirit'. Absolutely nothing happened, and absolutely no one present was surprised or concerned by the evident absence of the Holy Spirit! This was hardly the kind of event that Luke reports. Peter and John laid hands upon them and prayed, and at last they received the Spirit (Acts 8:14–17). It was immediately obvious to those praying and to those receiving prayer. They had been filled and they knew it. It's just the same for Christians today. We not only need to be filled with the Spirit, but we need to know when we have been.

Commanded to be filled

We have seen that being filled with the Spirit was part of the normal Christian life for the early Church. We must also recognise that it was not only a familiar experience but also expressly commanded. In his resurrection appearances Jesus placed great emphasis on the task of world evangelisation, but the command to be witnesses was accompanied by an instruction not to begin the Great Commission until the power of the Holy Spirit had come upon them: 'You are witnesses of these things. I am going to send you what my Father has promised; but stay in the city until you have been clothed with power from on high' (Luke 24:48–49). At the beginning of the book of Acts, Jesus twice speaks of the coming of the Holy Spirit. First he commands his disciples not to leave Jerusalem, but to wait for the promised gift of baptism in the Holy Spirit (Acts 1:4–5). Then he explains that their ability to be effective witnesses to the ends of the earth is dependent on the release of spiritual power, 'When the Holy Spirit comes upon you' (1:8). Quite simply, Spirit baptism is the prerequisite for effective witness. Jesus doesn't offer the Holy

Spirit as an optional extra for those personalities or churches who happen to like that sort of thing. Jesus's followers are expressly told by him that they need to be clothed with power from on high. The believer who refuses to ask to be filled with the Spirit is a disobedient Christian.

Some suggest that any talk about being filled with the Spirit creates second-class Christians. If this accusation were true, the apostle Paul would be at fault, since Paul's express desire for the Ephesians, which closely conforms to Jesus's perfect plan for his Church, is that every Christian should be filled with the Spirit: 'Do not get drunk on wine, which leads to debauchery. Instead be filled with the Spirit' (Eph. 5:18). The way that Paul uses the verb 'to be filled' is very significant. He uses the *plural form*, which means that his teaching is universally applicable. This is not an instruction just for leaders, or for those aspiring to some kind of 'higher' spiritual life. It is an inclusive and universal principle of godly living. There are no exceptions: this instruction comes to every believer.

Paul uses the *imperative form*. That means his teaching takes the form of a command. This is not an optional extra for the enthusiastic. Paul by no means introduces being filled with the Spirit as a tentative suggestion. On the contrary, it is a universal necessity of Christian discipleship. The weight of apostolic authority lies behind this command. Without exception, all Christians are commanded to be filled with the Spirit.

Paul uses the *passive form*. Being filled with the Spirit cannot be turned around to mean 'Get active and do the right things for Jesus.' As we saw in Jesus's final instructions, the effective service of even the apostles was made dependent upon first being clothed with power. We need to learn how to be in receiving mode, not just asking God to bless our best efforts, but humbling ourselves to receive the spiritual resources we simply cannot manufacture for ourselves.

Finally, Paul uses the *present continuous form*. The present tense means that the command cannot legitimately be shelved for some more convenient moment in the future. Paul is blunt and direct: *be filled now*. However, Paul doesn't teach that we need to be filled once and this will see us through for the rest of life. The way he expresses himself means both 'be filled now' *and* 'go on being filled'. When it comes to the Spirit, to be filled once is never enough.

The results of this filling are richly attractive. First Paul describes a vibrant release of open worship, in which we build one another up through psalms, hymns and spiritual songs (Eph. 5:19). Then he confirms that being filled with the Spirit leads to an enhanced God-awareness, not only in worship but in everyday living – 'making music in our hearts to the Lord' (5:19). As God fills us with his love, there will be an overflow of thankfulness back to God (5:20). As God serves us with his Holy Spirit, we can grow in the experience of serving one another in love, in the church, the family and the workplace (5:21–6:9). And finally, being filled over and again with the Holy Spirit will enhance our effectiveness in spiritual warfare (6:10–18). With so many life-transforming benefits, it is hardly surprising that Paul's teaching on the Holy Spirit takes the form of a universal command to every Christian to receive from God, in the present moment and throughout life: 'Be filled now and go on being filled with the Holy Spirit.' Those who ignore this unequivocal command have chosen to impoverish themselves and limit their usefulness to Christ.

Paul contrasts being filled with the Spirit with getting drunk (Eph. 5:18). The drunk is no help to anyone else: the Spirit inspires us beyond the limits of self-interest. When someone is drunk, others suffer: when someone is filled with the Spirit, others benefit. A drunk is 'under the influence' of alcohol: at Pentecost the believers were 'under the influence' of the Holy Spirit, who had taken unmistakable control of their lives. The New Testament doesn't suggest that the first Christians seemed permanently drunk to outsiders, but on the day of Pentecost no other explanation seemed more reasonable to account for their extraordinary exuberance. They were certainly filled with joy from somewhere, and people presumed it must have come out of a bottle! We need to feel slightly disturbed by Paul's careful comparison. This isn't a roundabout and religious way of saying, 'Don't drink too much.' Paul is not merely recommending respectable sobriety; he is urging Christians to surrender control, not to alcohol but to the Spirit of God. The strongest of liquors will sometimes claim to be life-enhancing, but only the Holy Spirit is truly invigorating – he comes to bring us the life of heaven.

If we talk about the 'fullness of the Spirit', the risk is that we can convey the impression that there is a point of arrival. We may appear to suggest that in addition to the promise 'once saved, always saved', we can also achieve the condition of 'once filled, always filled'. Nothing could be further from Paul's clear teaching, for he uses the present continuous tense to stress that we need to go on being filled. Whereas we are born again once for all, so that there is no such thing as being born again repeatedly, when it comes to the Holy Spirit what we need is not a single dosage but a regular refilling. A successful blood transfusion reinvigorates the system, which can then sustain itself without the need for further outside help. Living in the Spirit is more like running an all-American gas-guzzler, a car with an outsize thirst for petrol – we need to be filled up frequently.

Needing to be filled

When the evangelist D. L. Moody was asked whether he had been filled with the Spirit his reply was memorable: 'I have, but I leak.' When we fall into sin, the Spirit is quenched. As we minister to others, the Spirit flows from us, just as Jesus experienced power going out from him when he was touched by the woman seeking healing (Mark 5:30). Through tiredness and overwork we can become distant from God and in need of recharging. In all these ways and more, all of us continue to leak, and so we need to keep coming back to Jesus to be filled anew.

We not only need to be refilled because of leakage, but also because the Holy Spirit is always at work enlarging our capacity to receive. Ezekiel used the picture of an old cooking pot as a description of Israel, encrusted where it has not been cleaned properly over the years. I can picture similar pots from my scouting days many years ago, blackened on the outside from the fire and blackened on the inside where burnt food had not been scoured out properly. The blackened encrusting represented the sin which had disfigured Israel.

> Then set the empty pot on the coals
> > till it becomes hot and its copper glows
> so its impurities may be melted
> > and its deposit burned away.
> (Ezek. 24:11)

In a similar way, Peter uses the image of being purified like gold in the fire, the impurities being lifted from our lives (1 Pet. 1:7). As the Spirit works within us, he wants increasingly to scour the refuse out of our lives, and set us free, shining like new, as the people God made us to be. The more the Spirit works, the more inner space he creates. As he fills us, he creates the possibility of filling us even more.

The Spirit also enlarges our capacity to receive as he leads us into all truth (John 16:13). He increases our self-knowledge, revealing new ways in which we need to surrender ourselves to God, and he increases our knowledge of God, revealing more of his inexhaustible love for each of his children. As a result, he continually deepens what it can mean to be 'filled to the measure of all the fullness of God' (Eph. 3:19). There is always more for us to receive, and we are always being called to a deeper surrender to the Lordship of Christ.

Sometimes Christians lose their thirst for God. I have met a number of ministers and missionaries who have confessed to a terrible spiritual dryness that has crept upon them over the years. They lack an inner awareness of the presence and power of God, both for effective change in their own lives and for effective ministry to others. Our prayer ministry team have often prayed with visiting leaders who reveal that no one has prayed for them personally for many years. It is wonderful to see the living waters flow again into a life that has become a spiritual desert, but it is not God's intention that his people walk through endless years of aridity. At conversion we receive our first drink of the Spirit, but one sip is never meant to last a lifetime. The Spirit doesn't want to be an occasional Christian tipple, nor is he satisfied with topping up our lives from time to time. He wants to immerse us in himself. And he is looking for control of our lives, day by day.

Whenever Christians are not being filled with the Spirit, there is a terrible blight on the Church. Many Christian leaders have spelt out the enormous gap between normal church life at the end of the twentieth century and the spiritual dynamism of both the early Church and later periods of revival.

The dead, dry bones of the Church need the living breath of God. (J. R. W. Stott, *Baptism and Fullness*, IVP, 1975)

We inherit a situation today in which the Spirit of God has been quenched. Unnatural as it may be, the Spirit's power is absent from the majority of our churches. (J. I. Packer, *Keep in Step with the Spirit*, IVP, 1984)

The plain fact of the matter is that even the best evangelical religion bears little resemblance to the experience of the Apostles. We have conditioned ourselves not to notice this. (Gavin Reid from an article in the *Church of England Newspaper*)

Getting started

When we ask how to move from our ignorance to the fullness of the apostolic experience, we can stir up a hornets' nest. Everyone is agreed that our spiritual condition is often substandard, but many get hot under the collar the moment we try to bridge the gap. Talk about being filled with the Spirit is quickly understood to be 'pulling rank' on other Christians, by claiming a second-stage experience.

This whole difficulty arises from inadequate teaching about the Holy Spirit. The New Testament reveals that every believer receives the Holy Spirit at conversion. But when many of us were converted we were told little or nothing about the third person of the Trinity. The New Testament tells us to go on being filled with the Spirit. But many of us were encouraged to be suspicious, or to quickly change the subject, if anyone started talking about the Spirit. We were too wary to know much about him in theory, let alone in practice. The first apostles had no need to teach Christians to *start* being filled, or to be filled for the first time, because the first believers were brought into the faith properly. On profession of faith they were baptised with water, as an outward sign of living faith, and they also received the laying on of hands with prayer to be filled with the Spirit. For the first Christians, being filled didn't have to begin at some later time because it was as much a part of their Christian initiation as repentance and water baptism.

Our ignorance cannot prevent us receiving the Spirit in the first place. But it can trap us in a disastrous and unnecessary spiritual poverty. To suggest that we can be continually immersed in the life-transforming power of God, without ever asking to be filled and without any direct encounter or experience of the Holy Spirit, is nothing less than absurd. Although some who have genuinely been filled with the Spirit do fall into an unwarranted pride towards other believers, there is an equal and opposite pride among those who have never been filled and stubbornly refuse to admit it. Anyone who reduces discussion of being filled with the Spirit to what is wrong with someone else's theology is using a popular excuse to avoid the Spirit. Don't try to dodge the need to be filled. Don't try to use someone else's mistakes as a red herring. Unless this pride is broken, these 'got it all' believers do not have the remotest possibility of ever being filled with the Spirit.

Imagine that in the days when I used to commute to London, someone had bought me an annual rail season ticket in January, but forgot to tell me about it until July. I would have missed out on pre-paid journeys for six months, and nothing could make up for the lost opportunities. But as soon as I heard the good news I wouldn't want to miss out for a single further day. I would have to start somewhere, and it would be much better to start using the ticket in July than never use it at all. Abnormal circumstances require unusual solutions. In a similar way, we need to bridge the gap from our deficient and substandard modern, evangelical conversions to the early Christian pattern of teaching and experience of the Holy Spirit. Being filled with the Spirit should have been part of our Christian life from the day of our conversion. But some have been converted for many years without ever once asking to be filled. If you want to be filled, you've got to start somewhere, and it would be far better to start now than not at all. To put it bluntly, the sooner you start the better!

Taking the plunge

I want to describe a breakthrough experience of my own. Like a testimony of conversion, this isn't the only way God works, but it is the way he dealt with a particular person. For me this was a crucial experience that bridged the gap between a deficient or substandard modern conversion, and the biblical freedom to be filled and to go on being filled with the Holy Spirit.

It was mid-spring 1976 and the evening service at St Michael-le-Belfrey, York, was a communion service. That always meant a very special time of worship, 'lost in wonder, love and praise'. Suddenly David Watson suggested something new. After everyone had received the bread and wine, there would be an opportunity to come forward for prayer for special needs.

My heart warmed within me. It wasn't that I was aware of any particular need myself. But I had been used to rather traditional communion services: you queued in silence, waiting for a space at the rail; you received the bread and wine accompanied by formal words with no personal addition; and then you returned to your pew, carefully avoiding eye contact with any other worshipper. It felt so much more in harmony with the New Testament vision of the Church to have this time of personal encouragement and ministry.

As the singing group led us in quiet and sensitive worship, the first two or three went forward for prayer. It was only then that I experienced an overwhelming sense that God wanted me to go forward. I'd never felt anything quite like it before. It was as if someone had just switched on a powerful electric magnet in my stomach. But I distrusted emotions, and so I stayed firmly sitting in my pew. A few minutes later the feeling returned. I still didn't know for what particular need I was meant to go forward. Again I pushed the feeling away and sat tight. By now the time of ministry was nearly over. No one else seemed to be going forward. Then the powerful magnetic pull started for the third time. I had started the service feeling absolutely fine. Now I knew of a deep need within. I had resisted the prompting twice, but I knew I could ignore it no longer. If I resisted any more, I would return to my college room acutely aware of an unmet need. I simply had to go forward.

As I approached the altar rail where the elders were ministering, my need came into sharp focus. I knew I had received the Spirit at conversion. But now I realised I had been holding back from him. I realised too how little love I had for others, compared with the love of Christ. With a faltering voice I explained that I wanted God to fill me more with his Spirit and give me more of his love for others. I knelt down and hands were gently laid on my head. David thanked God for his promises about the Spirit and claimed them for me. As he prayed, I opened my heart and life to God deeper than I had ever dared or dreamed before. Then the prayer showed great wisdom. The request turned into thanks. Just as at conversion we can thank God that now we are saved, David thanked God that now he was indeed filling me in a new way, just as he had promised.

One friend told me afterwards that when I stood up to go forward I looked absolutely dreadful – more miserable than she had ever seen me. On the way back my face shone with a joy never seen there before. I was radiant with the Spirit of God.

That wasn't the end of my problems as a Christian. By no means! But it was an absolutely crucial moment of release. I lay in bed that night aglow in the Spirit. God was present with me in a way I had never known before. The indwelling of the Spirit was now a living reality, and not just an item of doctrine. For several hours I stayed awake, praising God and basking in this glorious immersion in the Spirit. You may think me very foolish when I tell you that, as I lay there, I wiggled my toes and with tears of joy I cried out, 'You are even there, right down in my toes!' The Holy Spirit had come, in fullness of love, power and joy.

I don't tell you my story to suggest that this is a blueprint experience for each and every Christian. That would be nonsense. I simply reproduce this testimony because I know that I am by no means the only believer for whom the necessary way to begin to go on being filled with the Spirit is through a decisive moment of new openness. To go on being filled, you have to ask to be filled for the very first time.

Be filled now

Being filled with the Spirit doesn't make you a superior Christian. All that we need to be saved is ours in Christ and so nothing can elevate us more in the eyes of God than the benefits of his Son's atoning sacrifice. Being filled with the Spirit cannot therefore create first- and second-class Christians: from the moment we first believe we are justified by faith. What we urgently need to do is to start living out in practice what has been available ever since the first moment of our conversion. The command to be filled is an invitation to obey the God of grace, and not turn away from the Holy Spirit after the very first sip. Being filled with the Spirit is not about what we can do for Jesus, but about what Jesus longs to do for us and through us.

The great crisis of the Church today is spiritual impotence: we cannot serve Jesus with the effectiveness he is looking for unless Christian believers are once again 'clothed with power from on high'. This supernatural power cannot be worked up by human effort, nor legitimately avoided by defensive explanations that we have already received the Spirit. We need to humble ourselves before our Saviour, asking Jesus to fill us, not just once but over and over again, with the Spirit of the living God.

FRUIT AND GIFTS

6

The Spirit of Holiness

Young children sometimes make enthusiastic gardeners. We heard of one toddler helping his dad. The father had sown seed to the end of a back-breaking row and at last he eased himself upright. His son had been very quiet, and he had been too absorbed and too stiff to keep looking up. Now at last he could give the child his full attention. Smiling proudly, the little boy held up a grubby hand. He wanted to give back to Daddy the seeds he had 'dropped'. A few years later that little boy will be sowing his own seed. After an hour or two he'll check whether they have sprouted. Within a week he'll dig some up, to see how they are getting on. A successful gardener needs patience, and not just with children and other horticultural pests. It's no good sowing, pruning or picking early. There's a right time to plant, and a right time to admire and eat. An immature fruit is no good to anyone if its lifeline to the tree is broken.

Just as a tree without sap can bear no fruit, without the Spirit there can be no fruit of the Spirit. When Martin Luther tried to save himself through religious works, he didn't only come to realise that he was guilty before a holy God. He also discovered his own 'impotence for good' and came to 'despair of his own strength'. In the same way, Jeremiah saw that we cannot transform ourselves. Just as the leopard cannot change its spots, we are all pre-programmed for sin. Jeremiah's conscience told him there must be a better way. The Spirit of God revealed how that would come about: 'I will put my law in their minds and write it on their hearts' (Jer. 31:33).

The Spirit brings new responsibilities as well as new privileges. The sons and daughters of God are also his new servants. Called to be in Christ, we are also called to be like him. Adoption is secure in what Christ has already done, but holiness requires a gradual heart change. The real test of this inner change is not on a Sunday because Christian behaviour can sometimes be put on with our Sunday clothes. If someone stands on your toe during the service are they a clumsy oaf? Never, at least out loud, on a Sunday! The critical moment is midweek. You're tired, waiting for a train or in a checkout queue, with no other Christian in sight, when a complete stranger stands on your toe. Are they a clumsy oaf *now*? Inner change is tested in our off-guard reactions. It may be an eruption that makes Vesuvius look like a failed firework, or it may be a split second of unrestrained negativity before we regain our composure. Instinctive reactions reveal the real condition of our heart.

When we have received the Holy Spirit, spiritual fruit is the natural outworking and demonstration of his presence. The Spirit bears fruit within us just as sap in springtime pushes out new buds. Fruit usually matures gradually. When Paul writes of fruit, he is suggesting gradual and organic growth rather than an instant and complete moral renewal. Our local garden centre had a display one autumn of newly developed bulbs for the gardener in a hurry. The foliage was perfect. Flowering was instantaneous. Genetic engineering has been making great strides but I didn't expect anything like this. They were ideal for the instant garden – so long as you like plastic. The unglamorous truth is that there are no instant answers in this life for genuine character transformation. A plastic veneer of superficial piety is no fruit of the Spirit. The Spirit wants to cultivate our character like a garden, and with our co-operation and surrender, we can enjoy a lifelong improvement in Christlikeness.

At the deepest levels of our characters, the Spirit wants to make us more like Jesus. He's an open heart surgeon, not a plastic surgeon. There may be setbacks and many operations, and progress won't always be apparent. But left alone we could never begin to renew ourselves, and so we must allow his deep remodelling the time it needs.

The target of holiness

If you want to hit a target, you need to know what to avoid. The Galatian Christians were free in Christ, but Paul warned them not to 'gratify the desires of the sinful nature' (Gal. 5:16). One part of every Christian wants nothing better than to give house room to sin, but our calling is to keep in step with the Spirit of holiness. The apostle Paul explains the Spirit's target of holiness and assures us that the Spirit is at work on the inside. He is very frank about the Christian's experience of inner struggle. But he never allows us to lose sight of the hope for inner renewal. Paul will be our chief guide to the Spirit of holiness at work within us.

Paul provides a catalogue of the 'acts of the sinful nature' (Gal. 5:19-21). They read like the stock list of a vast hypermarket of sin. There's something here for every kind of self-indulgence. They catalogue the tawdry world behind the scandal-scorched headlines of the gutter press: sexual immorality and debauchery, witchcraft and orgies, selfish ambition and fits of rage. Most people could never live their way through this comprehensive list of vices. But together they encapsulate what's wrong with our species.

Paul is as uncompromising as Jesus: both have no tolerance for sin. Tucked in with the excesses most of us avoid, there are a number of more socially acceptable, even 'respectable' vices. Party spirit, that is exclusive in-crowds, and arguments are found in the best of circles. A little envy and jealousy are surely standard fitments, not optional extras for society's outcasts! Paul doesn't include these less scandalous faults in order to play down the more outrageous sins in his catalogue. He does it to show that our sins, whether major or minor, whether denounced, tolerated or even admired by public opinion, all have the same source. Sin can be easy to spot in others. Jung observed that we often condemn most strongly in others the things we like least in ourselves. Whenever this happens, the Holy Spirit holds up the mirror of conviction and he shows us the sin that's our own. We cannot allow any 'acts of the sinful nature' to become acceptable through familiarity or regular use because all are pernicious to our spiritual vitality. 'No sin is small. No grain of sand is small in the mechanism of a watch,' wrote Jeremy Taylor.

Paul turns from the darker side of self to list the fruit of the Spirit. The fruit of right living doesn't come from what is sometimes called our 'better nature'. The best fruit comes from God's Spirit within us: 'The fruit of the Spirit is love, joy, peace, patience, kindness, goodness, faithfulness, gentleness and self-control. Against such there is no law' (Gal. 5:22-3). The Spirit produces fruit, not a variety of fruits. The word is singular, not plural. This needs to be emphasised time and again. Some Christians may be more keen on self-control than joy, more concerned with peace than patience, but that's not the way of the Spirit. If we find traces of two or three of these qualities in our lives, we cannot afford to settle back in complacency, for this isn't a list from which to pick and choose. The characteristics of the one fruit are like an apple's stalk and pips and flesh and skin. If even one is missing, the fruit is incomplete and deformed. The target of the Spirit is to produce all these characteristics in every Christian.

While there is not space in this book to consider each of these qualities in detail, we can recognise some general principles. It's difficult to analyse any one of these qualities in complete isolation from the rest. In practice they overlap, which underlines their indivisible unity as one fruit. *This fruit is immediately recognisable*, so that you cannot miss these qualities in someone. What is more, they are immediately attractive. These are the ideals behind countless new year resolutions. If you were asked what qualities are most desirable in the Christian life, Paul's list sums them up.

The fruit is designed for everyday living. These are not specialised qualities reserved for ministers or missionaries. The Spirit is given to all believers, and the same kind of fruit is meant to grow in every believer's character.

The fruit is beyond any law. No one can make kindness or goodness illegal. No law can make joy or patience compulsory. These are inner qualities which radiate in a new way of living. They cannot thrive as superficial add-ons to an unchanged life. Good works are the result of salvation, not a means of achieving it.

The fruit of the Spirit releases a new dynamic into how we relate to God, to others and to ourselves. For example, the Spirit writes upon our inner being the truth that we have peace with God through the cross of Christ. This peace that passes understanding can bestow a new peace with ourselves and also begin to permeate our relationships, bestowing a new peacefulness in our interaction with others. You only have to be with some people a few minutes before the peace, love or joy in their heart begins to warm your own. Spiritual fruit does us good and enables us to do good to others.

Every owner of an apple tree longs for its boughs to be heavy with fruit, like the master growers' orchards in the Garden of England.

All but the most degenerate people will at least sometimes yearn for a bumper crop of the qualities listed in the fruit of the Spirit. But only by the Spirit can we bear God's fruit.

The character of holiness

It's hardly surprising that love is the first quality in Paul's list of the fruit of the Spirit. Love is like the white light before it enters a prism: the other virtues are like the rainbow of fragmented light and together they make up love. Love is the sum of these godly qualities and the heart of the fruit of the Spirit. One life showed these qualities in perfect harmony. One life could be summed up by love. That, of course, was the life of Jesus, whose character was immediately striking and wholly admirable. The intensity of divine love within him meant that he saw behind the public face of others to their hidden needs. He loved not just the lovable, but everyone. He loved not for what he could gain out of it, but because he saw each man and woman through the eyes of God. Their needs came before his own well-being. When none of his disciples was prepared to wash the feet of the rest, Jesus the Master became the servant of them all. Tim Rice and Andrew Lloyd-Webber's Jesus Christ Superstar became exasperated with the demands of the crowds and cried out, 'Heal yourselves!' But the real Jesus kept on loving, kept on healing, even when his body must have ached with exhaustion.

Jesus said that a man's greatest love was to lay down his life for his friends (John 15:13). But God's amazing love went so much further. Jesus's self-sacrifice was made for us while we were yet sinners. It was for those in sinful rebellion, no less than the enemies of God, that Jesus was prepared to shed his blood (Rom. 5:8,10). Even when he endured the bone-wrenching agony of crucifixion, Jesus's prayer was not concerned with self-vindication – 'Show them I'm your Son!' Instead, other people stayed his top priority – 'Father, forgive them, for they do not know what they are doing' (Luke 23:34). The fruit of the Spirit as listed in Galatians composes an identikit picture of the character of Jesus.

Jesus's way of living could never be put on with a Sunday suit. His instincts were as selfless as his actions. His whole being resounded with the harmony of God's love. Holiness means living like Jesus, for the Father's intention is that Christians 'bear the family likeness of his Son' (Rom. 8:29 J.B. Phillips). As the fruit of the Spirit forms within us, we do indeed become more like Jesus, but it hardly takes much self-examination to know that this can only come about as a miracle. Suppose that Christianity was made illegal and this identikit picture was issued to make arrests: 'The police are looking for those with the family likeness of Jesus. They will be characterised by the following qualities: love, joy, peace, patience, kindness, goodness, faithfulness, gentleness and self-control.' We have to ask a searching question: would there be enough of a likeness for us to be convicted?

Paul longed for the Galatians to stop dabbling in fruitless attempts at spiritual self-improvement through the empty rituals of outward religious conformity. God's plan and Paul's desire was that 'Christ is formed in you' (Gal. 4:19). By grace we are in Christ. By the Spirit, Christ's character is formed in us. Desire for change tends to run far ahead of actual transformation, but that doesn't mean it is merely wishful thinking. Paul explains that we can take comfort in wanting to be more holy. Although such a desire cannot in itself guarantee rapid progress, it is a good sign that God is already at work, for it is the Spirit who makes the spiritual fruit and the character of Christ so attractive. Yearning for holiness is the prelude to personal spiritual growth, and the source of this aspiration is the Spirit of holiness at work within us: 'For it is God who works in you to will and to act according to his good purpose' (Phil. 2:13).

Sin is a smog which conceals our individuality under its grimy film. The Spirit wants to liberate our true individuality from the crushing sameness of sin. God loves the unique *you*. No one else can replace you. The Holy Spirit plans to set the real you free, for the more we become like Jesus, the more we enter into the freedom to become our real selves. The Spirit doesn't turn us into Holy Joes, all religious and out of touch. Jesus wasn't like a vicar in a television sitcom, he was more free, more fully alive, than anyone else in Galilee. Despite the great myth of the twentieth century, true freedom is not found in 'doing my own thing', because in my natural condition I am trapped in slavery to sin. True freedom is found in serving Christ, who has delivered us from this bondage to dull conformity and selfishness. The fruit of the Spirit is the character of Jesus, inscribed upon our lives.

The struggle for holiness

Growing in holiness is like riding a bike. If you stop pedalling, you fall off. The journey into holiness is nothing like a five-minute bike ride. It's more like cycling around the world. To get there you need to set an immediate target you can achieve, even it it's only the next village. But you shouldn't take your eyes off the final destination. If you see holiness as an effortless joy-ride, sooner or later you'll come crashing to the ground. The illusion of instant and easy moral perfection will lead in the end to despair: 'Either there's something wrong with me, since I cannot change myself, or maybe God has rejected me.' When we hide our struggle for holiness behind a slick Sunday smile, those who don't know us may think we find holiness easy. Lack of teaching on this struggle brings a harvest of needless problems. Disillusion is a tough price to pay for misplaced idealism. Anyone who plans to be a saint in a day risks being a hardened sinner tomorrow. The best fruit cannot be forced.

I once met a Christian who claimed to have stopped sinning. As a new Christian she'd had the usual problems, but now old sins were dead. There were still occasional lapses – admittedly she had committed a sin at the beginning of the previous week – but for the spiritually mature the journey into holiness had become an effortless joy-ride. I looked at God's standards and saw that holiness was an uncompromising mountain range. I looked in my heart and knew there could be no joy-ride into holiness for me. Sin doesn't just blemish with occasional lapses. It stains the very fabric of human life. Spurgeon once had breakfast with someone who similarly claimed he had attained sinless perfection. A jug was conveniently at hand; accounts of the story differ as to whether it was full of milk or water. Whatever the contents were, Spurgeon quickly poured them over this holy man's head in order to test his theology! His immediate fury made absolute nonsense of his claim to have graduated into a holiness beyond all sin. .

The apostle Paul's version of mature Christian living is quite different. He hasn't reached destination holiness. Nor is he coasting downhill. If anything, he is pedalling harder than ever: 'Not that I have already obtained all this, or have already been made perfect, but I press on to take hold of that for which Christ Jesus took hold of me (Phil. 3:12). Paul never loses sight of the Spirit's promised fruit, because he knows that Christ took hold of him to draw him into holiness. Neither does he forget his own continuing failings. Paul obviously feels this might be difficult for some of the Philippians to accept. It's as if he can anticipate their surprised reaction: 'If anyone has reached perfection, surely it's our apostle!' Therefore Paul repeats himself even more vigorously, stressing that he has definitely not arrived but, like a single-minded athlete, he is more determined than ever to go for it: 'I do not consider myself yet to have taken hold of it. But one thing I do: Forgetting what is behind and straining towards what is ahead, I press on towards the goal' (3:13–14). Just in case any Philippians now feel superior to Paul in his weakness, he adds, 'All of us who are mature should take such a view of things' (3:15).

Paul's description of a continuing struggle with sin alerts us to the continuing existence of our sinful nature, fighting within us all the way to the grave. Augustine described the same experience in the *Confessions*, his classic account of the struggle for holiness. He knew many inner conflicts before his conversion and in his early days as a believer. With the passing of years, he stopped committing those sins that had marred his younger days. However, as he grew closer to God he became more rather than less aware of the struggle within and the contamination that his sinful nature brought to his inner life: 'Heal me, in whose eyes I am now become a problem even to myself. That is my infirmity' (*Confessions* x:33).

The definitive biblical account of this inner fight with sin is found in Paul's letter to the Romans: 'I know that nothing good lives in me, that is, in my sinful nature. For I have the desire to do what is good, but I cannot carry it out. For what I do is not the good I want to do; no, the evil I do not want to do – this I keep on doing' (Rom.7:18–19). Many Christians have resisted the idea that this is a description of the normal Christian life, and so a number of interpretations have been developed that avoid this possibility. First, that this represents Paul's life as a Jew, living under the law before he came to Christ. Second, this represents his experience in a crisis of faith just prior to his conversion. Third, it represents his initial experience as a new convert, before he discovered the power of the Holy Spirit. Fourth, rather than representing Paul's specific experiences, this is a description of the typical experience of someone in any one of these categories. Fifth, it represents the experience of a carnal Christian, in other words someone who has come to faith, but has so far failed to overcome the power of their sinful nature through repentance and faith. All of these interpretations look to the end of chapter 7 as a description of an experience of liberation from this bondage to sin: 'What a wretched man I am! Who will rescue me from this body of death? Thanks be to God – through Jesus Christ our Lord!' (7:24–5).

All these interpretations have two things in common. They take seriously the struggle with sin in Romans 7, and they also bring to Romans 7 and 8 a chronological interpretation. That is, they assume that we initially experience the struggle of Romans 7, but subsequently we can graduate into the triumph of Romans 8. There is, however, an alternative interpretation, held by among others Augustine, Calvin, Spurgeon, Ryle and Packer, which concludes that Paul is describing two simultaneous perspectives on the Christian life. Not two phases, passed through in sequence, but two dimensions that we inhabit at one and the same time. On the one hand, in his mind he is now a slave to God's law, but at the same time in his sinful nature he remains captive to the law of sin (7:22–3). If we want to look at the Christian life from the perspective of the new provision of God, we need to turn to Romans 8. But if we want a clear understanding of the continuing presence of the sinful nature, and our continued and absolute dependence on Christ for grace and for strength in the fight for holiness, we need to turn to Romans 7. Conversion doesn't bring this fight to an end. In fact the fight is often intensified once we come to faith, because we have stopped living only for self, and the Holy Spirit is aiding us from within to become more like Jesus. We are no longer in helpless bondage to the sinful nature's every whim, but it fights every inch of the way in our struggle towards greater holiness. Anyone who confuses conversion or being filled with the Spirit with the impossible dream of achieving sinless perfection has failed to take seriously the teaching and experience of the apostle Paul. There is only one total cure for sin for any Christian, this side of the second coming of Christ, and that cure is death! Only in death will we be totally separated, once for all, from our old and sinful nature.

John Donne, the great poet and preacher, thought he was dying

in 1523, and was inspired to write a final confession. The sickness
left him, but his remarkable prayer about the struggle for holiness
is a poem of painful honesty but clear-sighted faith. It could be
written from the heart of every Christian:

A HYMN TO GOD THE FATHER

Will you forgive that sin, where I begun,
Which is my sin, though it were done before?
Will you forgive those sins through which I run
And do them still, though still I do deplore?
When you have done, you have not done,
    For I have more.

Will you forgive that sin, by which I've won
Others to sin, and made my sin their door?
Will you forgive that sin which I did shun
A year or two, but wallowed in a score?
When you have done, you have not done,
    For I have more.

I have a sin of fear, that when I've spun
My last thread, I shall perish on the shore;
Swear by yourself that at my death, your Son
Shall shine as he shines now, and shone before;
And having done that, you have done,
    I have no more.

The hope of holiness

Youth and idealism often go together. But can you teach an old
dog new tricks? Where the hope of holiness has never really found a
home, we tolerate too easily a life made up of little sins. We become
trapped by our character and resigned to our faults:

  'That's the way I am, and there's nothing anyone can do
    about it!'
  'Ours has always been a proud family.'
  'If there's one thing I have never been able to stand . . .'

No life is barren ground for the fruit of the Spirit. He who had the power to raise Jesus from the dead, has the power to change our lives. If God has begun a good work in you, don't let unbelief or old habits obstruct the advance of holiness. For example, our attitude to others can get in the way of the fruit of the Spirit. Is there someone you just don't get along with? Do they always seem to rub you up the wrong way? Don't just blame them for it. David Watson used to recommend that we turn the spotlight on ourselves: we shouldn't have a wrong way to rub up in the first place.

Matt used to think that the fruit of the Spirit essentially meant trying to do your best for Jesus. God gave the gift of new birth, but after that discipleship is all up to us. In the end Matt had to face an unpalatable fact: he couldn't change himself enough. Then he came to realise that the hope of holiness is this: he didn't have to change himself, at least not on his own. At last Matt began to pray in a new way, asking God not merely to bless him in his best efforts, but to help him in his weakness. Christ doesn't just offer forgiveness for past sins, he promises transformation in the present. The change in Matt wasn't total, but it was unmistakable. Now he worked to change himself no longer on his own, but in the Spirit's power. Six months later a friend returned from Canada. Her first comment to Matt said more than she realised: 'Hey, you've changed a lot! What's got into you?'

In the struggle for holiness there can be moments of sudden reversal. Paul warned that no Christian is above temptation (Gal. 6:1). But we need at the same time to keep hold of the hope of holiness. The inner transformations that the Spirit brings about can sometimes be swift and dramatic. As a teenager I smoked twenty cigarettes a day. Although I knew that smoking was bad for me, I didn't want to try to give up in case I couldn't break the habit. One day I suddenly realised that addiction to nicotine was working like a tyrannical little god in my life: if I ran out of cigarettes on a Sunday afternoon, I was prepared to walk some considerable distance to find a shop that was still open. Convicted by the Spirit, I asked for God's help and the power of smoking was broken overnight. At other times, the Spirit has brought change in my life not in a moment of dramatic crisis, but rather in a slow and painstaking process. There's not a single, universal method by which the Spirit breaks the chains and snares in our lives. Sometimes there's revolution, sometimes the gradual emergence of qualities more in line with Jesus.

Whether the fruit's development is fast or slow, we need to expect real change in practice. Paul makes it clear that sanctification, or growing in holiness, requires our co-operation. On the one hand, in conversion we have already 'died with Christ' (Col. 2:20), and yet it also remains true that we continually need to 'put to death . . . the earthly nature' (Col. 3:5). Although Paul can speak of the sinful nature as already crucified (Gal. 2:20), he also warns believers not to live in such ways as to promote its life anew, but rather to live to 'please the Spirit' (Gal. 6:8). The apostle is not playing with words. Our salvation is already complete at Christ's cross. But now we have to claim it and live in the light of it, not only in the surrender of conversion, but also in choosing to die to self, day by day.

Three biblical promises can do much to sustain our hope of growing in holiness. First, *temptation need not overwhelm us*: 'No temptation has seized you except what is common to man. And God is faithful; he will not let you be tempted beyond what you can bear. But when you are tempted, he will also provide a way out so that you can stand up under it' (1 Cor. 10:13). This verse denies the myth of irresistible temptation. We face what countless others have faced before. We are also promised that God is our helper in two vital ways. He knows how much each individual can take and he won't let us be steam-rollered by more than we can take. What is more, he provides a way out. In other words, even if we are careering towards sin like a lorry with failed brakes on the steepest of hills, there is always an emergency exit for us. We are no longer obliged to rush headlong into every sin with which we are tempted.

The second promise is that *forgiveness is always available*: 'If we confess our sins, he is faithful and just and will forgive us our sins and purify us from all unrighteousness' (1 John 1:9).

We don't have to pretend that we never sin, because in Christ there is no condemnation. 'Being holy means getting up immediately every time you fall, with humility and joy. It doesn't mean never falling into sin. It means being able to say, "Yes, Lord, I have fallen one thousand times. But thanks to you I've got up a thousand and one times"' (Helder Camara).

The third sustaining promise is that *we no longer need to be dominated by our sinful nature*: 'You, however, are controlled not by the sinful nature but by the Spirit, if the Spirit of God lives in you' (Rom. 8:9).

Mature Christians don't stop sinning, but they grow in understanding of their own need to be helped into greater holiness. In the power of the Spirit they continue the struggle, and as they press on the fruit will steadily grow. As J. H. Newman observed, 'To obtain the gift of holiness is the work of a lifetime.' The journey into holiness may not be easy, and it will certainly not be completed in five minutes or even five years. But the struggle is worth continuing, in the power of the Holy Spirit, for growth into holiness is making us fit for heaven, where sin will be no more and where we shall delight in the 'glorious freedom of the children of God' (Rom. 8:21).

The pursuit of holiness

If we are going to make any progress in holiness, we need to understand that the Spirit requires self-denial. This is hardly a fashionable or immediately appealing statement in our self-indulgent age. A friend of ours faced strong sexual temptation. Many Christians have struggled with this in past generations. Many have demonstrated that while it may not be easy, it remains possible to deny lust and keep in step with the Spirit. But ours is the instant generation: 'Without sex, no fulfilment, and why wait for fulfilment?' This kind of attitude is popular, but ultimately empty and deceitful. Sadly, self-denial was too much for our friend. He chose sex, not the Holy Spirit. If we are truly followers of Jesus we need to remind ourselves that the supreme demonstration of self-denial is his crucifixion. When legions of angels could have been summoned to his rescue, Jesus still chose the way of the cross.

Jesus wants his disciples to pursue holiness with every fibre and sinew of our being, and so he calls us to take up our cross daily and follow him (Luke 9:23). Someone using a plough with oxen had to concentrate in order to cut straight lines through the earth. If distractions kept enticing them to look over their shoulder, the result would be a shambles, a field unfit for sowing, disfigured with zig-zag furrows. Jesus used this illustration from everyday Galilean life to issue one of his most severe warnings to his followers: 'No one who puts his hand to the plough and looks back is fit for service in the kingdom of God' (Luke 9:62). John Chrysostom was a golden-tongued preacher of the fourth century who didn't hide the need for the discipline of self-denial from his congregation. He made no apology for the fact that training in holiness can be hard work:

> The younger athletes practise on the bodies of their comrades the attack that one day they will have to launch on their opponents. Let this be a challenge to you. Practise yourself in the discipline of true religion. You see many Christians unable to resist the paroxysms of anger, and others set on fire by the flames of lust. Practise resistance against such passions. (John Chrysostom, *Thirty-third homily on St Matthew*)

The Spirit also requires sacrifice. For some Christians, their possessions are all-absorbing. Their lives are so full, there's no room left for holiness. Others are dedicated to a career that demands nothing less than total commitment. Some end up living fragmentary and self-contradictory lives. As one businessman expressed it, 'At home it's God first, family second and work third, and in the office the order is reversed.' Before fruit can be grown successfully, undergrowth and dead wood need to be uprooted and priorities need to be sorted out: 'Some persons, laden with wealth . . . make no progress nor come to harbour, because they have not the courage to break with some whim, attachment or affection . . . Yet all they have to do is to set sail resolutely, cut the ship's cable, or rid themselves of the sucking-fish of desire' (John of the Cross, *The Ascent of Mount Carmel* 1: xi:iv)

The Spirit is working within us for continuous growth in holiness, but this growth is not automatic. There's an old story that when Leonardo da Vinci was painting *The Last Supper*, he looked for a model for Christ. He is said to have chosen a choirboy from a church in Rome. Pietro Bardinelli was known as a boy 'lovely in life and features'. Years passed, and the painting was nearly finished. Only Judas Iscariot was left to paint, and Leonardo now wanted a model whose face was hardened and twisted by dissolute living. At last he found a Roman beggar with a face so villainous that he shuddered at the sight of it. He hired the man and painted his face.

When he was about to pay and dismiss the model he commented, 'I've not yet found out your name.' The reply astounded him: 'I'm Pietro Bardinelli, who was your model for Christ.'

The Spirit wants an increasing harvest of holiness, not a bowl of yesterday's fruit. Some old people's faces are lined with laughter. Every wrinkle seems to smile. To be with them makes you feel closer to God and glad to be alive. Others grow more stubborn and glum with every year, till their features set into a fixed scowl – 'Where habits are sown, a character is grown.' The Holy Spirit's transformational purposes never cease: he is always at work to change us further into the likeness of Christ: 'And we . . . are being transformed into his likeness with ever-increasing glory, which comes from the Lord, who is the Spirit' (2 Cor. 3:18).

We need to examine ourselves. In the time since my conversion, what has life done to my Christ-likeness? Jesus died: is my sinful nature being put to death in him? Jesus rose: does his resurrection shine out through the changes in my life? Jesus reigns: am I confident in the Lordship of Jesus, not only in how I worship but also in how I live? There's no substitute for the fruit of the Spirit. Nothing else can make you more like Jesus. Nothing else brings you more into line with the ways of God. The Spirit of Christ is the Spirit of holiness. Holy is his name and holiness is his intention in every believer. Give the Spirit freedom to change you, give him time and give him all the co-operation you can.

A few years ago I spoke at a national Baptist congress in Denmark. The platform was beautifully decorated, not only with plants, but also with trees in large pots, and on each tree was a lavish crop of apples. From a distance the bumper crop of beautiful fruit was most impressive. Closer inspection revealed that the trees were not fruit-bearing at all, and the apples were held in place with wire and tape. In that instant of discovery, those trees became a stark symbol of warning to all Christians. Outward religious conformity is never enough. The fruit of the Spirit can only grow where the sap of the Spirit is flowing freely through our inner being. It's no good hanging fruit on dead trees.

7

Popular excuses for avoiding the gifts of the Spirit

There is a song that some Christians could easily sing:

> If you take the gifts road,
> And I take the fruit road,
> I'm sure I'll get to heaven before you!

All who begin to divide the united work of the Spirit begin to separate themselves from the one Spirit of Christ. Just as in chapter 4 we faced up to popular excuses for avoiding the Holy Spirit, we now turn to popular excuses for avoiding his spiritual gifts.

Excuse One: The spiritual gifts died with the first apostles

The absence of the spiritual gifts from many churches today would be no problem at all, if they really had died out with the apostles. There is only one problem with this theory: there is no historical evidence that it happened. Those who want to believe that the gifts have long since passed their sell-by date refer to Paul's letter to the Corinthians: 'Love never fails. But where there are prophecies, they will cease; where there are tongues, they will be stilled; where there is knowledge, it will pass away. For we know in part and we prophesy in part, but when perfection comes, the imperfect disappears' (1 Cor. 13:8–10). The cessationist theory proposes that the apostles needed certain gifts to launch the Church. Once the apostolic foundation had been laid, and the books of the New Testament had been written, certain spiritual gifts became redundant and simply ceased to be given or used.

It takes a great deal of ingenuity to read into the passage the obsolescence of the spiritual gifts at any time before the second coming. If you are convinced of this already, you may try to read it into the text, but it would have been very hard indeed for the Corinthians to have taken that meaning from what Paul actually wrote. Paul looks forward to a time when imperfection will be replaced with perfection: we shall see face to face instead of a poor reflection; we shall know God fully, even as we are already known. There is only one stage of human history that Paul would describe in such terms: the return of Christ and the manifold perfections of resurrection life in heaven. Paul's point is that while love will last throughout eternity, the time for the spiritual gifts is here and now. For as long as we live with our present, imperfect and incomplete knowledge of God, the gifts of the Spirit are an indispensable asset to the body of Christ.

When Paul lists the necessary elements for regular worship in the next chapter (1 Cor. 14:26), prophecy and tongues find their natural place alongside preaching and singing. If Paul really had known that the spiritual gifts were only for the first generation, it would be quite extraordinary that he did not give more help for the churches to plan ahead. At the very least, we might have expected him to sort out the short-term spiritual gifts into a separate list, and explain the adjustments that would need to be made to the style of worship once these gifts had passed out of use.

Paul not only advises the Corinthians in the right use of spiritual gifts, he specifically encourages them to seek more gifts and to be 'eager to prophesy' (1 Cor. 14:39). His enthusiasm can hardly please today's devotedly hard-line anti-charismatics. Far from laying plans for the time when the gifts would cease to exist, Paul actively encouraged the gifts to flourish.

We still need to ask whether the gifts did drop out of existence at the end of the apostolic age. Just imagine the correspondence that would have flown between the churches faced with a miracle of such magnitude. As they pieced together the evidence they would have discovered than on exactly the same day in every fellowship, there were no more prophecies, no more healings, and no more speaking in tongues. Further careful enquiries would have revealed that this was the very day on which the last surviving member of the original apostles had died. It would have been a remarkable miracle if the last remaining apostle had taken the spiritual gifts with him at his death. We would expect an enormous amount of comment in that generation's sermons and letters to this overnight transformation of Christian worship. But of such evidence there is no trace.

Either the gifts died with the first apostles or they did not. This is not an issue for half measures. The evidence we can assemble from the early generations of Christians is not restricted to one or two unusual incidents. Nor are those who speak of spiritual gifts in any way unreliable witnesses. The most respected leaders from the mid-second century to the early third century speak with one voice. They lived close to the age of the apostles, and would surely remember any decisive moment when the gifts dropped out of sight. Instead, they testified that the Spirit was still active in the Church, and still bestowing his gifts.

Justin Martyr was a leading Christian apologist in Rome. He was executed in 165 for refusing to sacrifice to pagan gods. In one of his evangelistic books he described the continued operation of spiritual gifts: 'Even to this day the gifts of prophecy are alive among us: you can see among us both men and women who are endowed with gifts of grace' (*Dialogue with Trypho*, 82).

Eusebius, the renowned church historian of the fourth century, quoted Irenaeus, Bishop of Lyons, who died some time after 180. Irenaeus cites the spiritual gifts in the Church as a continuing demonstration of the fact that Jesus was not a conjurer but a genuine miracle-worker:

> Some drive out demons really and truly, so that often those cleansed from evil spirits believe and become members of the Church; some have foreknowledge of the future, visions and prophetic utterances; others, by the laying on of hands, heal the sick and restore them to health; and before now, as I said, dead men have actually been raised and have remained with us for many years . . . Similarly, we hear of many members of the Church who have prophetic gifts and by the Spirit speak with all kinds of tongues, and bring men's secret thoughts to

light for their own good, and expound the mysteries of God.
(Eusebius, *History of the Church* 5:7)

Irenaeus stressed that the complete range of gifts was still available to
the Church and could be found in regular use: 'In fact, it is impossible
to enumerate the gifts which throughout the world the Church has
received from God . . . Freely she received from God, and freely she
ministers.' Faced with such evidence, Eusebius concluded: 'This will
suffice to show that diversity of gifts continued among fit persons till
the time I am speaking of' (Eusebius 5:7). Origen (AD 185–254) was
also able to report that he had often witnessed healings, prophecies
and deliverance ministry.

In the mid-second century, a number of church leaders were
considered prophets, including Hermas, Polycarp and Melito.
Hermas explained how to discern true prophecy and encouraged
Christians to 'trust the Spirit who comes from God and has power,
but do not believe the earthly, empty spirit at all' (*The Shepherd
of Hermas*). We still have a copy of a sermon preached by Melito,
Bishop of Sardis, in which at one moment he is preaching in his
usual style, then suddenly the tone is transformed. Christ begins to
speak through him in words of prophecy:

Who will contend against me? Let him stand before me. It is I
who delivered the condemned. It is I who gave life to the dead.
It is I who raised up the buried. Who will argue with me? It is
I, says Christ, who destroyed death. It is I who triumphed over
the enemy, and trod down Hades, and bound the Strong Man,
and snatched mankind up to the heights of heaven. It is I, says
Christ. So then, come here all you families of men, weighed
down by your sins, and receive pardon for your misdeeds. For
I am your pardon. I am the Passover which brings salvation. I
am your life, your resurrection. I am your light, I am your salvation, I am your King. It is I who brings you up to the heights
of heaven. It is I who will give you the resurrection there. I will
show you the Eternal Father. I will raise you up with my own
right hand. (*Homily on the Pascha*, Papyrus Bodmer 13)

As a young Christian, Augustine thought that spiritual gifts were
no longer given to the Church and dismissed the possibility of healing

miracles in his own generation. Later he was forced to change his mind, as a result of examining the evidence for himself:

> For when I saw, in our own times, frequent signs of the presence of divine powers similar to those which had been given of old, I desired that narratives might be written, judging that the multitude should not remain ignorant of these things. It is not yet two years since [we began the list] ... And though many of the miracles which have been wrought have not, as I have the most certain means of knowing, been recorded, those which have been published amount to almost seventy at the hour at which I write. (Augustine, *The City of God* 22:8:21)

If the gifts did not evaporate overnight, we need to consider other less reassuring explanations for those times in church history when they have not been utilised. Through the first four centuries we see a gradual decline of spiritual vitality. The more respectable the Church became, and the more ordained men claimed exclusive control of Christian ministry, the less the spiritual gifts were desired and given.

The excesses of a breakaway group called the Montanists stirred up a reaction that killed off the spiritual gifts in many churches. Some of their prophets slipped into extremism and began to claim that they alone possessed the Spirit of God. They tried to make their own prophecies supersede the New Testament, and decreed exactly when and where the second coming would take place. The official Church over-reacted in typical fashion, restricting the ordinary people more than ever and making spiritual gifts the sole preserve of the clergy. In time only ordained men could preach; a little later only ordained men could prophesy. As a result the distinctive gift of prophecy steadily disappeared from Christian worship. Tertullian (*c.* AD 160–215), a brilliant North African defender of the faith, eventually gave up on the mainline Church and joined the Montanists. He said it was the bishops, not the Spirit of God, who had taken the gifts away from the Church, by gradually reserving more and more spiritual gifts for the clergy alone.

Not everyone agreed with the official policy. As late as the fourth century, Bishop Cyril of Jerusalem still thought that those being baptised might receive the gift of prophecy. However, he avoided rocking the boat too much by stressing that he did not think it very likely in practice! John Wesley summed up this sad story: 'The grand reason why the miraculous gifts were so soon withdrawn was not only that faith and holiness were well-nigh lost, but that dry, formal, orthodox men began even then to ridicule whatever gifts they had not themselves; and to decry them all, as either madness or imposture.'

If all the genuine gifts had died with the apostles, we would have to reject outright the witness and experience of Justin and Irenaeus, Melito and Augustine. The best you could say was that the gifts they experienced were delusions. At worst, you would have to say that all their gifts, and indeed all spiritual gifts exercised across the generations of the Church of Christ have been nothing other than demonic counterfeits. John Owen, the seventeenth-century Puritan theologian and Vice-chancellor of the University of Oxford, had a far more balanced view than that. Owen did not think that all spiritual gifts were available in his own generation. But his willing acceptance of the doctrine of the sovereignty of God meant that it was quite impossible for Owen to exclude the possibility of the future re-emergence of all the gifts: 'It is not unlikely but that God might on some occasions for a longer season put forth his power in some miraculous operations, and so he may yet do and perhaps doth sometimes' (John Owen, *Pneumatologia*).

The gifts did not die with the apostles. This popular excuse for avoiding the Spirit simply will not stand up. The witness of history is enough to prevent anyone from taking cover behind this excuse. The theory of cessationism sprang up much later to explain away the absence of spiritual gifts, and it flies in the face of the historical evidence. The gifts were still being enjoyed by the Church many decades after the first apostles had died, and those same gifts are being poured out freely by the Holy Spirit upon the worldwide Church today.

Excuse Two: The gifts are too risky

The New Testament writers insist that churches must test spiritual gifts (1 Thess. 5:19–22). Their proper use cannot be taken for granted. It is possible to imitate genuine gifts, whether to impress or mislead. Many non-Christian religious groups have their own forms of prophecy, tongues and healing. Jonathan Edwards, the eighteenth-century American theologian, shrewdly observed that 'a work of God without stumbling blocks is never to be expected. God gives the genuine gifts. Imitations are either man-made or demonic.' Some Christians have dealt with this kind of danger by setting up an exclusion zone around their churches, making them spiritual gift-free areas.

The gifts do become risky where there is not proper leadership. No one should try to usurp leadership because they happen to exercise an impressive gift. Excitability or a domineering attitude are no substitutes for the Spirit's still, small voice of calm. We must not over-react. It would be quite irresponsible to ignore the biblical instruction to test spiritual gifts. But no good can possibly be achieved by overstating the risks and avoiding the gifts altogether. What is more, leaders are incapable of giving an effective lead if they are not exercising the gifts themselves: if any leaders are not Spirit-filled and hold a dismissive attitude to certain gifts, those gifts are very unlikely to be manifested in any meetings that they are leading. Just as a middle-eastern shepherd walks in front of his sheep rather than driving them from behind, the leaders provide a secure framework for the gifts to be used by being ahead of the church. Just as a river will not rise higher than its source, a church will not go deeper into renewal than the leaders are prepared to go.

Leaders need to work closely together and to be open to the Spirit's prompting. They need a thorough grasp of Scripture to test any word of prophecy. The gift of discernment needs to be discovered and developed. Above all, leaders need to be filled with the love of God. First, so that their love for the fellowship gives them the courage to speak out if a 'gift' is not from God. Second, so that they give correction in a way that will build up and reassure any who make mistakes, ensuring never to crush them. I came across one leader who claimed that he accepted the gifts in principle, but thought he had never heard an authentic prophecy in his life: his sweeping dismissal showed no spiritual discernment. It is hardly surprising that tongues and prophecy have never surfaced in any service he has ever taken.

Perhaps the most abused gift is preaching. All kinds of peculiar people have preached all kinds of strange messages. That doesn't mean we abandon preaching. On the contrary, it means that those who cherish the gift of preaching are all the more determined to proclaim the Word of God, faithfully and accurately, with clarity and with passion.

Jesus was not only a wonderful preacher, he also frequently healed the sick. He didn't stop using the gift of healing because some tricksters pretended they could do it too. He didn't refuse to heal unless people had never tried another healer. He didn't ask them to sign a contract before they were healed that would guarantee his apostles would have exclusive rights and total control over publicising the healings. Jesus knew the problems. He knew all about people's mixed motives. But healing power had been given to express and demonstrate God's love for us. And so Jesus showed no reluctance to heal.

In the same way, the Spirit still gives his gifts, despite the risks. They need testing, and the Spirit encourages that. But the best way to guard them from abuse is not to forbid them, just in case an imitation slips through the net. We guard them best by putting them into action, so that the gift of discernment is informed by good experiences of the gifts being used properly and profitably. As has often been said, the wise response to misuse is not disuse but right use. John Owen summed up the attractiveness of the early Christians, despite the risks attached to making active use of the spiritual gifts: 'And I had rather have the order, rule, Spirit, and practice of those churches which were planted by the apostles, with all their troubles and disadvantages, than the carnal peace of others in their open degeneracy from all these things' (*Pneumatologia*).

If the risks really were too big, the Holy Spirit would never have released the spiritual gifts into the body of Christ. He would have left us to serve Christ by making the best of our natural abilities. Far greater than any risk attached to using the gifts is the risk of not using them at all. If we ignore the gifts and leave them out of our regular church life, we are actually choosing to ignore the teaching and practice of the New Testament. The church that uses the popular excuse that the gifts are too risky is really saying that God himself is too risky: their tidy religious world would be far too disrupted if God turned up at their services or if the gifts that he gave to build up the church were actually put into action. The sober truth is this: whenever we reject spiritual gifts, we also reject the Giver. Now that is a risk that I am certainly not prepared to take!

Excuse Three: What's the use of speaking in tongues?

The gift of tongues still has many Christians puzzled. In their churches, this gift is only mentioned in suspicious or dismissive tones. Their leaders prefer never to speak about tongues at all, and if they do, their emphasis is entirely upon the dangers and abuses. The only thing that is guaranteed about tongues in many churches is that this is one gift that no one will ever be allowed to use.

I was converted in such a church. What made things worse was the fact that the only church in town where the gift was encouraged went right over the top, concentrating on tongues more than anything else. They completely ignored the practical instructions Paul provided for the Corinthian church. Paul said that two or at the most three should speak in tongues at one meeting (1 Cor. 14:27). He insisted on the importance of interpretation (14:27). He even encouraged the tongues-speakers to hold back when non-Christians were present, putting seeker sensitivity above total freedom of expression in public worship (14:22–23). In giving these instructions, as a keen tongues-speaker himself, Paul is showing us the essential nature of the gift. It is never 'ecstatic utterance', as the New English Bible extravagantly mistranslated the Greek word used in the New Testament that simply means 'tongues'. Such a phrase implies that the speaker is completely out of control, in a state of frenzied enthusiasm. On the contrary, Paul understands the gift to be under the control of the tongues-speaker, who makes active choices about whether to use the gift in a particular setting.

The trouble was that the misuses I met served to confirm my instinctive prejudice against the gift, and I was inclined to write off tongues altogether. That's like finding one cracked egg in your weekly shopping and vowing never to buy anything from any supermarket ever again. My problem was serious: I accepted in theory that God gave the gift, but in practice my heart was so set against it that if anyone as much as mentioned tongues I expected problems.

Many people request the gift of tongues to enrich their prayer life.

I eventually prayed for tongues too, but for a very different reason: if you reject a gift, you reject the giver. My gut reaction was so opposed to tongues that it was only by praying specifically for it that I could be delivered from my prejudice. Only by this deliberate repudiation of my deep-rooted prejudice could I complete my repentance, stop quenching the Spirit, and be fully open to God.

That was twenty years ago. Ever since I received the gift of tongues, I have found that it keeps on developing, which should come as no surprise. After all, preaching or any other gift matures with experience and practice. Similarly, when we learn a foreign language, it takes time for fluency and confidence to grow. So what is the value of tongues? Because some people struggle with the very idea of such a gift, and can see no point in it at all, the explanation that follows will be very practical and personal.

Very often when I am praying for someone whose needs are acute I have little idea how to pray. I may sense an underlying need, but not be able to discern it clearly. Or I may know their needs all too well, and feel almost overwhelmed by the difficulty of their circumstances. When we feel an urgent need to intercede, but we don't know how to pray, the Spirit helps us in our weakness, enabling us to intercede beyond the limits of our own understanding and to enter into the sublime, heavenly prayer of Jesus – 'at the right hand of God and interceding for us' (Rom. 8:34). One of the main ways in which the Spirit takes us into this prayer 'too deep for words' (8:26) is through the gift of tongues.

I usually pray in tongues when I am involved in prayer ministry, whether privately or at the end of a meeting. As I pray in this way, beyond the limits of my own understanding, I often find that the Spirit then provides me with a Scripture, a prophetic word, or a prayer in English that really opens the person up to whatever Jesus wants to do in their life at that particular time. Similarly, when I am not sure what decisions to make, I find that praying in tongues, often while walking my dog on Wimbledon Common, is a way of coming to God to seek the wisdom that I lack. Prayer in tongues is also very effective faced with those who are demonised. After deliverance ministry people often describe an intensified sense of the power of the presence of God when those ministering to them have prayed in tongues.

Tongues is an effective way of expressing submission to God.

It's a bit like musicians warming up in the orchestra pit: as I pray in tongues I am asking God to tune me up, and make sure that I am once again brought into harmony with my Master. Before preaching, I like to spend some time on my own praying in tongues. At conferences I try to go for a solitary walk to make space for this kind of preparation. Jesus explained that without him we can do nothing, but if we abide in him we shall bear much fruit. Even so, as I pray in tongues, as well as in English, I want to express a profound sense of yielding, humbling and dependence upon God, as I seek a fresh anointing with supernatural love, wisdom and power. Without the touch of God, we preachers have nothing to offer except mere human insights and opinions. Truly evangelical preaching is more than reliable exposition, it is truth on fire.

Tongues is very helpful in times of acute pressure, when life gets on top of us. The burden may be too much anxiety and fear; it may be that we have so much work to get through and so little time to do it; some kind of conflict may threaten to engulf us; or someone's attitude, behaviour or words may have cut us to the raw. An unkind comment can bite deeper than ever intended, and there are times when it doesn't help to show our reaction. I can recall an occasion when I prayed in tongues while travelling home from a difficult meeting, expressing a pain deeper than words could say. The Spirit helped me to tell the Father about the hurt and then he moved me beyond it. I found I was now praying not for myself, but for the one who had hurt me. Left to myself, I would have been tempted to hold on to my hurt and become angry or resentful. As I prayed, the Holy Spirit delivered me from pain, drew me back into God's love, and enabled me to forgive.

Above all, tongues releases a new language of love. Some couples have private ways of talking together. They make up special phrases that express their intimacy and devotion, but would seem meaningless or just plain silly to anyone who overheard them. Tongues can give that kind of intimacy to prayer. Similarly, when someone has visited a sensational beauty spot, and they try to describe what it looked like and how they felt, they often lapse into incoherence, spluttering apologetically, 'I'm lost for words: I just cannot put it into words.' Tongues comes into its own when ordinary words fail. Prayer can be lifted into new dimensions of intimacy when, from the depths of our hearts, we begin to express love and adoration beyond the limits of normal language.

I am not for one moment suggesting that tongues is the only means of praying in these ways. But it certainly helps! These personal experiences demonstrate at least some ways in which those who pray in tongues really are able, in Paul's explanatory phrase, to 'edify themselves'. Tongues enriches our openness to God. It makes us more available to receive his love and his power.

The phrase 'gift of tongues' allows for a great deal of variety. Paul indicates that not all tongues are human languages such as those understood by visitors to Jerusalem on the day of Pentecost – 'each of us hears them in his own native language' (Acts 2:8). Alongside 'tongues of men', which means recognisable human languages, Paul also refers to 'tongues of angels' (1 Cor. 13:1). Most believers experience a growth in fluency in a new tongue, as we exercise the gift in private and also pluck up courage to use it when praying with others. What is more, we can receive more than one tongue, praying in unmistakably different languages at different times, facing different kinds of opportunity and need.

All good gifts bring risks and temptations and tongues is no exception. Three common risks are legalism, self-indulgence and pride. Legalism arises if we feel that praying in tongues is strictly necessary in order to receive power. This could lead to an exaggerated fear that a day without tongues would automatically be a day of disaster. Self-indulgence is when the sheer pleasure and intimacy of praying in tongues threatens to squeeze out prayer in English. Some have a similar problem with worship songs, or with praying for themselves or even with an ever-growing shopping list of prayers for others. Too much time on any one dimension of prayer risks distorting our whole walk with God. Tongues complements other kinds of prayer: it is not designed to make them obsolete. Pride is always trying to take up squatter's rights in our hearts, disfiguring with false superiority our attitudes towards other Christians. The Greek word for 'spiritual gifts' is *charismata*, from the root *charis* which means grace. The New Testament consistently recognises that they are always and exclusively gifts of grace. The gifts are never a reward for what we have done, or an excuse to look down on those who don't have the same gifts as us. They are the Spirit's gifts of undeserved love to the Body of Christ.

The apostle Paul provides practical guidelines for making the most of tongues. He stresses that tongues is a genuine gift of the Spirit, and so should never be forbidden, because all God's gifts are good (1 Cor. 14:39). Christians should never presume to pick and choose among the spiritual gifts according to their own preferences or prejudices. To do so is to risk putting out the Spirit's fire in our personal lives and in our local church (1 Thess. 5:19–20).

Paul encourages those who have received the gift of tongues to pray for the gift of interpretation, because this maximises the usefulness of the gift they have already received (1 Cor. 14:13). Where there is no interpreter, Paul instructs tongues-speakers to keep quiet, which serves as a further incentive to them to begin to exercise the gift of interpretation (14:28). 'Interpretation' naturally conveys a wide breadth of communication beyond literal, word-for-word translation: an interpretation may convey the sense of the original tongue, addressing God in prayer or praise, but it may just as legitimately provide a prophetic response to the original prayer, or even an English version of a prophecy given originally in tongues.

Paul describes praying in tongues as 'praying with my spirit', while regular prayer is termed 'praying with my mind' (1 Cor. 14:15), and he insists that both are invaluable. He also speaks of *singing* 'with my spirit' and 'with my mind' (14:15). Paul leaves this singing free from the restrictions he applies to praying in tongues. While corporate praying in tongues is not permitted – no more than three in a meeting, one at a time, with interpretation (1 Cor. 14:27) – Paul puts no equivalent prohibition on corporate singing with, or in, the Spirit. Everyone who has enjoyed the exquisitely beautiful harmonies of such singing, some using their native languages, others praying in tongues, all united in the adoration of God, will know why this experience can be nothing less than a glorious foretaste of the worship of heaven.

Paul and Luke are the New Testament writers with most to say about tongues, and Luke makes it plain that tongues was a very common gift among the first Christians. Paul goes further, for he explicitly declares his own eager desire that every single believer might speak in tongues, even though he is even more keen that everyone might prophesy (1 Cor. 14:5). We need to be careful not to make more of tongues than the apostle, for tongues is not the most important gift of the Spirit. At the same time we must be careful not to despise a gift that was invaluable to Paul. Although in his public ministry Paul's priority was intelligible communication in the language of the people (14:19), tongues none the less played a critical part in his ministry. Some modern Christians write off the Corinthians as a tongues-mad church. But Paul confidently claims that in personal prayer he uses the gift of tongues more than any of them (14:18).

Once I couldn't understand the gift of tongues, but I was sure I didn't want it. Now I wouldn't be without it. It's by no means the most important spiritual gift, but it certainly is a wonderfully enriching way to pray. If anyone is hostile, in their heart or mind, towards tongues or any other New Testament gift, it is vital to surrender that prejudice before God. If we reject one spiritual gift, we reject the giver of them all, and that's very serious. I'm reminded of the health warning on cigarette packets. *Despising the gift of tongues can seriously damage your spiritual health.*

Excuse Four: We don't need prophecy any more

Two prophecies in the book of Acts reveal how important this gift was in the early Church. Agabus, one of a team of prophets visiting Antioch from Jerusalem, foretold a severe famine over the entire Roman world. Without waiting for the disaster to strike, the Christians at Antioch immediately provided aid for the poorer churches of Judea (Acts 11:28-30). It was also from Antioch that Paul and Barnabas started their church-planting journeys, in obedience to another prophetic word: 'While they were worshipping the Lord and fasting, the Holy Spirit said, "Set apart for me Barnabas and Saul for the work to which I have called them"' (Acts 13:2).

Prophecy was a very familiar gift in the early Church, exercised by many believers from time to time. We know that the gift was used by women as well as men, because Luke reports that Philip the evangelist had four daughters who all prophesied (Acts 21:9). Those whose prophetic gift was particularly well developed and widely recognised became known as prophets (Acts 11:27; 1 Cor. 12:28; Eph. 4:11). Some of these prophets travelled from place to place (Acts 11:27), others became leaders within local churches.

At Antioch, for example, the leadership team was composed of prophets and teachers (Acts 13:1).

We don't have a record of the vast majority of the prophecies given in the early Church, which means that the first Christians didn't bother to collect them in written form. Because they don't have the lasting authority of Scripture, most prophecies can safely be forgotten once they have made their immediate impact. Prophecy is subordinate to Scripture, and is given by the Spirit to complement Scripture, just as the Spirit inspires the words of a preacher or songwriter. Prophecy is much more than foretelling. It is more often a word of comfort, rebuke or guidance, addressed to the immediate needs of a particular fellowship or individual. In general it is best not to pass round prophecies too widely. They are usually given for particular occasions, not for all time, and have one-off relevance. In all that the New Testament says, there is absolutely no indication that prophecy would be no longer needed after the completion of the New Testament. True prophecy does not claim for itself the same status as Scripture, and certainly never pretends to replace Scripture. According to the New Testament, prophecy is an invaluable gift, which can greatly enrich the life of a local fellowship.

Prophecy continued to have a considerable impact in the early Church. In AD 70 the Romans finally lost all patience with the troublesome inhabitants of Jerusalem. They massacred many Jews, tore down and burned the city, and destroyed the temple. Amazing though it may seem, the local Christians had advance warning of this disaster. Eusebius records that they obeyed a prophetic warning to pack their bags and escape before the disaster: 'The members of the Jerusalem Church, by means of an oracle given by revelation to acceptable persons there, were ordered to leave the city before the war began . . . To Pella those who believed in Christ migrated from Jerusalem' (*History of the Church* 3:35).

Many modern Christians would not think this kind of prophecy to be credible or possible. If such a warning was received in many churches today, we must doubt whether many would be prepared to abandon their homes in a similar way. However, I recently had an opportunity to meet a Christian leader from the Latvian community in Brazil. Early in this century Latvian Christians received prophetic warnings of a disaster coming upon their homeland and they decided to seize an opportunity to emigrate before the bloodshed began. Their great-grandchildren in South America today are a living witness to the benefits of taking prophecy seriously.

Not every experience of prophecy in the early Church was so positive. Strange ideas were sometimes promoted under the guise of authentic prophecy. Some Christians in Thessalonica had given up their work to wait eagerly for the second coming: someone had claimed prophetic authority for the conviction that Jesus was guaranteed to return within a few days or weeks. Paul wrote quickly to repudiate and correct this teaching (2 Thess. 2:1–3). But he was also concerned that they should not miss out on genuine prophecy in future as a result. Rejecting all prophecy out of hand is just as foolish as drinking in someone's words without testing them. Paul explained to the Thessalonians how to make the most of prophecy. On the one hand he tackled the problem of cynicism and warned them never to treat prophecy with contempt. At the same time he wanted to protect them from gullibility, instructing them that every prophecy needs to be tested. What is more, he stressed that those prophecies that are good need to be held on to, valued highly and taken very seriously (1 Thess. 5:20–21).

The Holy Spirit will never take offence when we test prophecy. On the contrary, the witness of Scripture reveals that the Spirit wants prophecy to be tested. Only in this way is real prophecy separated out from its poor imitations. The Spirit who gives the gift of prophecy also gives the gift of discernment, and so he is actively at work within the Church to help us identify and benefit fully from his genuine gifts. There are five main tests for prophecy:

(i) Is it in line with Scripture?
The Bible is God-breathed, and the Holy Spirit will never contradict what he has already and definitively revealed in the Word of God (2 Tim. 3:16). When the gift of prophecy is rightly used, it cannot distract from Scripture, but rather enhances the Bible's supreme authority.

(ii) Does it glorify Jesus as Lord?
The Holy Spirit's constant delight is to bring glory to Jesus (John 16:14). If someone speaks words that distract from or denigrate Jesus in any way, they cannot be delivering a genuine prophecy.

Similarly, it is only by the Spirit of God that Jesus is confessed as Lord (1 Cor. 12:3). If we hear this declaration in a prophecy, we know the spiritual source is good. If this confession is denied, the words cannot be inspired by the Holy Spirit.

(iii) What is the credibility of the prophet's daily life?
The New Testament teaches that home life is an acid test for being able to take on public ministry (1 Tim. 3:2–7; Titus 1:6–9). If your household is unruly, you should not become a leader in the Church. It would be absurd to demand sinless perfection, but the more someone's daily life is in a mess, the more reason to be cautious about any prophetic word they bring.

(iv) What is our instinctive discernment?
It would be absurd to try to endorse a prophetic word on the grounds that it feels right, if it has already failed the tests of conforming to Scripture and glorifying Christ. On the other hand, a well-intentioned effort might pass these tests with flying colours but still not be a genuine prophecy. It might be inappropriate at that particular moment, or completely bland and lifeless. For a prophetic word to be weighed thoroughly, this inner, intuitive evaluation is therefore also essential.

(v) Does it come true? (Jeremiah 29:9)
Not all prophecy includes an element of foretelling, and so this test is not always relevant. What is more it has a great advantage but also a great weakness. The advantage is that our evaluation of the prophecy becomes cut and dried: either the prediction is fulfilled or not, beyond any dispute or shades of interpretation. The disadvantage is that we may have to wait some time before this evaluation can be made. Things become still more complicated when we realise that Old Testament predictions are generally conditional: if you continue in your ways, this judgment will follow, but if you repent, blessing will be poured upon your land. Therefore, if conditions are attached, and we fail to meet the conditions, we cannot reject the prophecy as false simply because the positive but conditional promises have not been fulfilled. However, if a prophet provides an unconditional prophecy that remains unfulfilled, this should prompt great caution in how we evaluate that person's prophecies in future.

Two more tests were added by the early Church which indicate that they came across some rogues and fakes. Prophets often had a travelling ministry, and the custom was that they were given hospitality by the churches they visited. However, a fraud might decide that the food wasn't good enough or the pay was too mean:

> No prophet speaking in the Spirit who orders a table spread will eat from it unless he is a false prophet. (*The Didache*)

> The man who only imagines he has the Spirit ... accepts payment for his prophesying, and if he does not get it he does not prophesy. It is impossible for a prophet of God to act like this. (*The Didache*)

Jeremiah gave some stern warnings about using prophetic terminology casually. He complained that so-called prophets inflate their own ideas as words from the Lord (Jer. 23:26). Every time a prophet has a dream he announces it as a divine revelation (23:28). They 'wag their own tongues', but have the arrogance to keep on saying 'the LORD declares' (23:31). Israel therefore glibly distorts and cheapens the 'words of the living God' (23:36). When everyone dresses up their own thoughts in grand language, 'every man's own word becomes his oracle' (23:36). Jeremiah warned that God will punish those who say lightly 'thus says the LORD', bringing everlasting shame upon them and their households (23:39–40). Jeremiah's warnings are severe and remain timely, but we cannot call for a complete ban on such ways of speaking: although Jeremiah recognised the dangers of such a direct prophetic style, he was none the less still prepared to declare, 'Thus says the LORD . . .' We need to be cautious and never casual, but so long as we take account of these warnings, some prophetic words are still best expressed in the direct style of Jeremiah.

Anything done in public worship needs wise leadership. To many people, whatever is said at the front of a church is more or less infallible. Without proper public testing of prophecy some less informed and gullible believers may be at the mercy of whatever is said. Such testing needs to be done at several levels. In many churches those who believe they have a prophetic word will approach the service leader first to seek clearance to speak it out. Whether or not this is done, the leader of the meeting will need to make an initial evaluation. If there is real uncertainty what to make of a word, the leaders of the church, together with any who are recognised as prophets, will need to make a more thorough assessment and response. Individuals need to be encouraged to lay hold of the word for themselves when it is personally applicable, and if the word has significance for the whole church, the congregation will in due course need some kind of opportunity to own the word, embracing it as part of the church's overall vision.

Sometimes the Spirit speaks to us an entirely personal message, and we bless no one by turning private revelation into public prophecy. There's a simple test to use during a prayer meeting if you think words of prophecy may be forming within you. Ask God to guide you by having a particular person pray next. Sue did this, and John, the person she had named, did pray next. Sue wasn't convinced that easily, and explained to God that John often prayed aloud, so could God confirm his guidance by having John pray again! When God promptly arranged things as requested, Sue surrendered her hesitations and a new prophetic ministry was begun. All prophecies need testing by the fellowship, so never claim that your guidance makes you infallible. But if you pray in this way, the Spirit will make it easier for you either to take the plunge and speak out, or to keep quiet until you really do have something useful to say.

I remember one occasion when a 'prophecy' ticked off a fellowship for creeping half-heartedness. So far so good. But then the speaker gave dire warnings of a severe judgment, held back until now like flood waters behind a dam. God's patience had run out, the dam was about to burst, and waters of judgment would be unleashed upon the fellowship with dire consequences. The opening words were both biblical and relevant, but by the end there was no room left for the God who doesn't snuff out a flickering candle nor break a bruised reed (Isa. 42:3; Matt. 12:20). 'No condemnation for those who are in Christ' seemed completely forgotten. One elder thought this was so obviously over the top that nothing more need be said. Fortunately the others disagreed: false prophecy that contradicts the gospel of grace must be gently but firmly weeded out.

We can all make mistakes. On one occasion I was quite sure that I had received a prophetic word that might cause difficulties in a particular meeting. The burden of the responsibility to be faithful to God in a demanding and pressured moment made me neglect the golden rule of always testing potentially controversial words with other leaders. Because I failed to submit the word to others, asking them to discern not only whether the content was godly but also whether the timing was right, the importance of what was being said was lost, and the impact was not clarity but confusion. Every wise leader will learn to submit their prophetic words, especially the difficult ones, to the discernment of other leaders.

Prophecy takes many different forms. At one church weekend God gave me a clear and detailed picture of a series of concentric walls that needed to be breached, followed by a river that needed to be crossed. It seemed to speak of a series of obstacles the church needed to overcome for God's purposes to be fulfilled among us. A few days later I attended a leaders' prayer meeting, where a Swiss Christian I had never met before stood up to give a prophetic word. He spoke in German, with each phrase translated into English, and I could hardly contain my astonishment as, step by step, he described exactly the same vision. When the description of the scene was complete, an extra phrase was added: 'And your church is to go to the Muslim peoples.' At that time a missionary couple in our church were considering the possibility of a move to Cairo, and the prophetic word was one more link in the chain, not only for their personal guidance, but also to establish in the church a strong sense of responsibility and commitment to stay involved in their vision. God authenticated the particular guidance by providing the identical vision through an entirely independent prophetic word.

Where prophecies provide personal direction, they need to be treated with wisdom. No one should rush into action on the basis of a single prophetic word. In fact such words are normally best kept at arm's length until there is independent confirmation of the guidance. However, when they are handled wisely, such prophecies are a wonderful source of encouragement and inspiration. On one occasion a note was dropped through our letter box from a complete stranger. He had been flying on Concorde when the Holy Spirit came upon him and he became convinced of the need to pass on a prophetic word to me. The message was that the days of preparation were ended, for now God was raising me up to new things and was saying, 'Do not hold back.' The covering letter that came with this prophecy was almost apologetic, recognising the inherent dangers in sending a prophetic word to a complete stranger, or in taking too seriously a word from someone you have never even met. None the less, the word was so astonishingly timely, given the exciting new ministry opportunities that had recently come my way, that I had every confidence in accepting it as a genuine word from the Lord.

Some personal words are more scary. At one conference a church leader rushed up to me after a time of ministry in which I had prayed for him. The prophetic word spoken over his life had been so precise to his circumstances that he was terribly worried in case I now knew too much about him. Relief flooded his face when I assured him that, having given such a word, my normal practice is promptly to forget whatever has been said. It is vital that prophetic words do not result in anyone claiming and abusing inappropriate power over someone else's life.

I recently heard of another church where a visiting speaker brought prophecies for many individuals within the fellowship. The elders were so astonished by the uncanny accuracy of these words that they concluded that their minister must have briefed the speaker in advance. As a result, they advised the next church meeting that their minister should be removed from office for such appalling breaches of confidence. When it became clear that the minister had done nothing of the sort, and that it was the Spirit of God who had revealed the secrets of men's and women's hearts, it was the suspicious elders who were duly removed from office!

Paul taught that prophecy is a greater gift than tongues (1 Cor. 14:5). It is an outstanding gift for building up the fellowship (14:4) and can also have a powerful evangelistic impact, even causing outsiders to 'fall down and worship God, exclaiming, "God is really among you!"' (14:25). Paul's policy was that two or three prophets at most should speak in any one meeting (14:29). He explained that the thread of a single prophecy can pass from one person to another, and if this happens, the first prophet should sit down and let the next continue (14:30). In all his advice, Paul makes it clear that Christian prophets remain in control, and do not enter an extreme ecstatic state where they are incapable of stopping a torrent of prophetic utterances.

Paul wanted every Christian to pray in tongues, but his desire was much greater that everyone might prophesy (1 Cor.14:5). While he urged believers to desire eagerly all the spiritual gifts, he particularly encouraged them to desire the gift of prophecy (14:1). At the end of his chapter of invaluable practical advice on the use of tongues and prophecy, Paul reiterated the priority he wanted them to embrace: 'Therefore my brothers, be eager to prophesy . . .' (4:39).

Moses shared Paul's conviction that prophecy is an invaluable gift of God. In days long before the outpouring of the Spirit at Pentecost, Moses expressed a passionate longing for the new age of the Spirit and a universal release of the gift of prophecy: 'I wish that all the LORD's people were prophets, and that the LORD would put his Spirit on them!' (Num.11:29).

The Church has not and cannot outgrow the gifts the Holy Spirit provides. If we are going to be empowered and effective we need to make full use of every resource that God has given his people. If we are serious about being biblical Christians, we need to take to heart the longing of Paul and Moses. We need to desire, pray for and encourage a mighty release of prophetic gifts, and all the other spiritual gifts, in every local church today.

8

Gifts to build the body

One of the most exciting footballers today is Eric Cantona. When he came back from his Kung Fu ban, Manchester United became championship contenders and began winning most matches once again. Anywhere near goal he's dangerous. A good striker takes his chances. But a great striker makes chances out of nothing. Before a shot looks even possible, the ball has hit the back of the net. During Manchester United's 1995–6 Double triumph, they gained twenty-one points from league matches where Cantona was the only scorer, and in the FA Cup Final the only name on the scoresheet was his.

For a few short years the top soccer players are worth their weight in gold. Crowds cheer, the autograph hunters lie in wait for them, and other managers try every inducement they know to persuade them to agree a transfer. Every year, in playgrounds up and down the country, countless schoolboys dream they are playing as well as the latest football hero, whether that's Pele or Bobby Charlton, Alan Shearer or Roberto Baggio. However, while one Eric Cantona at the top of his form is magnificent, we would pity any manager with eleven players in his squad who had exactly the same skills and identical temperaments. Not even eleven clones of Pele would make a real team, although eleven George Bests would certainly make a party to remember ... To make a successful team, everyone has to be prepared to work together, but you can't afford to lose sight of individual skills. Many people are convinced that the reason the England manager Glen Hoddle didn't get many more caps as a player is that the managers were unwilling to inject into their rigid game plan the unpredictable flair of the best English playmaker of his generation. Paul applied this same principle of teamwork to the effectiveness of the human body and the Church of Christ. It is precisely because there are so many different parts, with so many different functions, that the human body is so adaptable and can achieve so much.

Gifts for the body

Paul writes about the Church as the body of Christ in four letters: Romans, 1 Corinthians, Ephesians and Colossians. Many other metaphors are used to describe the Church, including the Family of God, the Bride of Christ and the Temple of Living Stones, but the Body of Christ was one of Paul's favourite ways to portray the Church. This no doubt resulted in part from his dramatic conversion, in which the risen Christ revealed that to injure the bodies of Christians, through beatings, imprisonment or death, is to do injury to Christ himself: 'Saul, Saul, why do you persecute me?' (Acts 9:4).

Speaking about the body of Christ was not just a pep talk for a disunited fellowship. Paul didn't dream up this comparison simply to inject some team spirit into the Corinthians. It's not just that the Church at its best functions something like a body. When we surrender our lives to Christ we actually become a living part of the body of Christ, and we need to learn how to be integrated in practice with our fellow believers: 'For we were all baptised by one Spirit into one body' (1 Cor. 12:13).

When Paul calls the Church a body, he doesn't have in mind an out-of-condition armchair spectator, slouched in front of the television when the sports programmes are on. Rather, he is picturing the Church like a well-trained athlete, every muscle and sinew in top condition and doing its work to the full. Sadly, the Church has often seemed more like a bus than a body. There are seats in rows on which the vast majority sit back passively, while the person at the front does all the work. Like an old-fashioned bus conductor, there is even someone who comes round to collect the money.

God's masterplan for his Church to function as a body is found in the gifts of the Spirit. Depending on how you count them, the total number of different spiritual gifts found in the New Testament has ranged from nine to twenty-seven. The Spirit of God is creative and can never be tied down to a rigid formula. In his gifts he delights in variety. Some Christians have counted nine gifts in 1 Corinthians 12:8–10 and have then concluded that this was Paul's definitive list. These can be sorted into three categories: gifts of knowing (discernment, wisdom and knowledge), gifts of doing (healing, miracles and faith) and gifts of speech (prophecy, tongues and interpretation). All these gifts are clearly commended by Paul, and follow his affirmation that while the gifts are diverse, they are all provided by the same Spirit of God. Although he doesn't bother to sort them into three neat categories, the real problem with this tidy arrangement of the nine spiritual gifts is that Paul actually provides two other lists of gifts in the same chapter that contain different selections of gifts.

Paul's second list comes at the end of his explanation that each Christian has at least one gift for use within the body (1 Cor. 12:27–8). He omits several gifts from his first list – discernment, wisdom, knowledge, faith and interpretation – and adds instead the gifts of helping others and administration, together with mention of apostles and teachers. This second list begins with an order of priority for the first four, but then Paul gives up numbering them. It seems likely that on the one hand Paul is emphasising that certain gifts are foundational, but at the same time he acknowledges the impossibility of enumerating every single spiritual gift, let alone setting them in a comprehensive order of priority.

We can also detect a distinct emphasis in the way that certain gifts are listed in terms of the task the gifts enable various kinds of leader to fulfil: apostles rather than those with apostolic gifts, and similarly prophets, teachers and workers of miracles. Paul doesn't suggest that these four are official positions in every local church that someone has to be slotted into, like so many designated places on a parochial church council or eldership. On the contrary, they require gifts that can only be received from the Holy Spirit. But Paul is clearly hinting at distinctive categories of gifting for various kinds of leadership.

The third list contains seven gifts (1 Cor. 12:29–30). The first five from the second list are retained, and so is tongues. Interpretation of tongues is reinserted after tongues, but helping others and

The Five New Testament Lists of Spiritual Gifts

Romans 12:6–8	1 Corinthians 12:8–10	1 Corinthians 12:28	1 Corinthians 12:29	Ephesians 4:11
		apostles	apostles	apostles
prophesying	prophecy*	prophets	prophets	prophets
				pastors
teaching		teachers	teachers	teachers
				evangelists
serving				
encouraging				
contributing to others				
leadership				
showing mercy				
	wisdom			
	knowledge			
	faith			
	gifts of healing	gifts of healing	gifts of healing	
	miraculous powers	workers of miracles	workers of miracles	
	discerning spirits			
	tongues	tongues	tongues	
	interpretation		interpretation	
		helping others		
		administration		

* Prophecy is second in every other list, but sixth in this one.

administration are left unmentioned. The distinctive feature of this third list is the series of rhetorical questions: 'Do all . . .? Do all . . .?' The Corinthians must have all been hankering after the same gifts, because the plain inference of the questions is that the Spirit delights in diversity. Far from the Spirit giving everyone the same package deal, the mark of a church truly open to the Spirit is an abundant variety of gifts.

Turning to Romans 12, we find once again that a list of spiritual gifts follows teaching on being the body of Christ, in which different members have different functions. What is more, just as 1 Corinthians 12–14 makes love central to any discussion of the body and the gifts, the second half of Romans 12 centres on Christian love. This list records seven gifts: prophecy, serving, teaching, encouraging, contributing to the needs of others, leadership and showing mercy. Six of these seven do not appear in the first list in 1 Corinthians 12, which certainly undermines any claim that the nine gifts found there represent the definitive list of spiritual gifts. All but prophecy and teaching don't even get mentioned in the Romans list at all. There's no indication that Paul is listing only the gifts exercised in the church at Rome. That's extremely unlikely, for the simple reason that Paul hadn't visited that church yet. Nor does Paul suggest that this or any other list contains the most important gifts. What is clear is that God has lavished upon us the riches of his grace (Eph. 1:7–8) and the unsearchable riches of Christ (Eph. 3:8). With such love beyond limit, an exhaustive list of spiritual gifts is clearly impossible, and no attempt to provide such a list can be found in the New Testament.

Gifts of grace

The minister who took our marriage service gave some very useful advice. He said it was important always to treat your partner as someone very special. Otherwise, with passing years, someone once loved deeply can begin to feel treated like another piece of furniture. One suggestion he made was to make a habit of surprising each other with little gifts. Such love-gifts are just one way of keeping a relationship fresh and growing. Often parents surprise their young children with love-gifts. The child's delight is worth more than words can say! As children become more knowing, presents start to become expected. A surprise is anticipated by a demand. At that stage parents begin to worry, quite rightly, about spoiling the child. Gradually the supply of presents dries up.

Many adults only expect presents at Christmas and birthdays. In some jobs, Christmas presents from friends and family can seem almost swamped by the 'gifts' from companies investing in your goodwill. Most of us aren't very good at either giving or receiving presents. If someone so much as compliments us, we try to shrug it off – 'Oh, it was nothing!' And if someone gives us a present, we wonder what might be the catch.

Just as salvation is a gift from God, he delights to shower his adopted children with love-gifts. As we have already recognised, the gifts of the Spirit are described by Paul as *charismata*, which is derived from the Greek word *charis* and means 'gifts of grace'. God doesn't provide his gifts as a perk for dedicated service or a reward for being religious. He doesn't give gifts because we deserve them or because our birthday has come round. He gives gifts, quite simply, because he loves us.

Some years ago, two people sitting with me in a tightly packed bus began talking about spiritual gifts. I must admit my ears pricked up. One girl had recently prayed in tongues for the first time. She found the gift greatly enriched her prayer life, but she had a problem. Far from tongues making her arrogant, she thought her friend Mandy far more 'committed' than she was. So why had God given her the gift, when Mandy was far more deserving? We need to drive home the New Testament message time and again. The gifts of the Spirit are never a reward. They are never God's stamp of approval on good attempts at self-improvement. We never ascend a league table of spiritual gifts and experiences, according to how well we are progressing. Paul says we have different gifts, not according to some merit table, but 'according to the grace given us' (Rom. 12:6). God's gifts are always love-gifts.

The Spirit is not restricted to spectacular gifts. The various lists in the New Testament mix together gifts which grow out of natural aptitudes, like teaching or administration, with those like healing or tongues, which seem much less predictable. John Owen, the seventeenth-century Puritan, helpfully summed up these two kinds of gifts: 'gifts such as consisted in extraordinary improvements of the faculties of the minds of men' and gifts 'such as exceeded all the powers and faculties of men's minds' (*Pneumatologia*). The gifts which grow out of natural aptitudes are no less given by the Spirit and no less important to the Church than the others. There is no rigid division between a 'spiritual' part of life, and a 'secular' part. Whether the Spirit grants a new gift or empowers a natural aptitude, a spiritual gift in action is always something very special. 'When God uses a person's gifts, it is anything but natural' (Edward Schweizer).

The Spirit is concerned with every part of the life of the Church, and he is involved in every activity of individual Christians. We need to recognise that the church administration and finances depend on the gifts of the Spirit as much as, for example, a ministry of healing. There is nothing worse than leaving the Spirit out of day-to-day affairs, as if we can cope there by ourselves, or as if he's a far-removed chief executive, who really doesn't want to be troubled with mundane details. This doesn't mean that natural gifts can be ascribed casually to the Spirit, but it does mean we can offer him 'what comes naturally', and ask him to enrich and transform it.

There is no suggestion in the New Testament that we should ever behave as if the gifts don't exist, simply leaving it to divine discretion whether any spiritual gifts at all are released in our local church. When the Thessalonians poured cold water on the gift of prophecy they were sternly rebuked by Paul: to despise spiritual gifts means to 'put out the Spirit's fire' (1 Thess. 5:19–20). There is nothing wrong with desiring a spiritual gift, so long as we want to use it for the Church, and not for our own glory. In fact Paul specifically instructs the Corinthians to follow the way of love and 'eagerly desire spiritual gifts, especially the gift of prophecy' (1 Cor. 14:1). How can they reasonably do this unless they request the gift in prayer? We don't say it is presumption to pray that we might be born again. An earthly father delights to hear the requests of his children. How much more does our heavenly Father desire to hear our requests, especially when he has revealed that he delights to shower his gifts upon his Church.

One well-known preacher is reputed to have prayed earnestly for three solid months for the gift of evangelism. He became one of the most greatly used evangelists of his generation. Of course, to ask is not the same as to demand. Earthly fathers don't take too kindly to being endlessly pestered with requests for more presents. To ask humbly is right and proper: to try to insist is always foolish. Our heavenly Father reserves the right to know better than us what gifts we need. He also reserves the right to say, 'No, my child.' When it comes to the spiritual gifts; the Holy Spirit is in charge, and 'he gives them to each one, just as he determines' (1 Cor. 12:11).

Different together

The early Church was an extraordinary group of people. People of startlingly different backgrounds mixed together. Jews would not allow Gentiles into the main temple areas, for they would defile the sacred place. Yet Jews and Gentiles were united in the New Israel. Slaves were someone else's possession, yet they worshipped alongside freemen and slave owners in the new family of the Father. Jewish men thanked God in regular prayer that they hadn't been born as women. Yet men and women, irrespective of race and social standing, all needed saving just as much, and they could all be united as equals in Christ: 'There is neither Jew nor Greek, slave nor free, male nor female, for you are all one in Christ Jesus' (Gal. 3:28).

It was inevitably not always easy to sustain this radical new way of living. Paul urged the Roman Christians not to let the world 'squeeze you into its mould' (Rom. 12:2 J. B. Phillips). Deep-rooted attitudes and prejudices need inner transformation through the Spirit's renewing power. The attitude Paul tackles first, in the very next verse, is pride: 'Do not think of yourself more highly than you ought, but rather think of yourself with sober judgment, in accordance with the measure of faith God has given you' (12:3). One aspect of this problem was class consciousness and snobbery. Later Paul urges the Romans to 'be willing to associate with people of low position' (12:16). The one who conforms to the world clings to the things that make him, in his own eyes, superior to others: nationality, colour, job, background, education, wealth, athleticism, or even how long you've been a Christian. Some were thinking too highly of themselves – 'I do wish the slaves would hold their own service.' 'We wouldn't want Gentiles like that living in our neighbourhood!' As a result, Paul had to remind such believers that their only true status was as sinners saved by Christ.

Before Paul turns to social divisions, he looks first at divisions to do with attitudes to spiritual gifts. The one who conforms to the world exploits the gifts he has been given to boost his own status and maximise his own advantage. Some were clearly thinking too highly of their gifts, treating them as their personal property: 'My gifts are really spectacular and showy!' 'I'd like to see this church try to get by without me!'

Paul confirms that different believers have different gifts, but there is no link between particular gifts and any claim to special status. In the first-century Church, there was no top table for VIPs. Any gift can become a target for misplaced pride. The best solution is not for the Spirit to avoid giving gifts, but for our underlying attitudes to be transformed. To the Corinthians, Paul makes the same point three times over, to stress the great variety of gifts from the single divine giver. There are *various* kinds of gifts, *various* kinds of service, and *various* kinds of working, but there is only *one* Spirit, *one* Lord and *one* God (1 Cor. 12:4–6).

God intends us all to be different and through the spiritual gifts he gives us different functions. Each Olympics pushes back the frontiers of human achievement. What was beyond reach fifty years ago has now become necessary in many events just to qualify for the final. Some years ago the Russians were rumoured to have discovered their gold medal sprinter, Valeri Borzhov, by asking a computer to identify the perfect physical build for the 100 metres. However, over 3,000 metres, Borzhov would have fared no better against today's Kenyan middle-distance runners than a slender gymnast would in the shot-put against the giantesses of Eastern Europe. Not even television's Gladiators can be equally good at every event. We have to find our particular God-given strengths. Just as no one is equipped for every sport, no one has ever received every gift of the Spirit.

In the Winter Olympics of 1984 the world watched entranced as Jayne Torvill and Christopher Dean danced the Bolero. They were in a class of their own and perfect scores were almost guaranteed. To this day television programmes still repeat the remarkable footage of those moments of triumph. At the same time one of the less glamorous Olympic events was in progress. This was the luge, in which contestants race down a steeply curved ice track, cornering at speeds that would be lethal on level ground in a car. They lie down a few inches above the ice, on a tiny sled which is the only thing between them and certain disaster. To compete successfully in this event requires extreme fitness, but a certificate of insanity also helps. Victory in the women's event that year went to an East German. She was the ideal shape and weight for staying on the sled at maximum speed, weighing in at a burly thirteen stone. Imagine the Lady of the Luge partnering Christopher Dean in the Bolero! She was a great champion, but no one can excel at everything! In the same way, if ever we try to do everything in the Church, without identifying our particular spiritual gifts, we court disaster.

Not only are there many different gifts and contributions to the body of Christ, but Paul also recognised that not all of them are equally eye-catching. It's the same in soccer: a mid-field dynamo will be in the thick of the action for ninety minutes, whereas a goalie may make less than half a dozen saves in the whole match if his team is dominant. The goalie needs the temperament to wait alone in his area, attentive to the game at the other end of the pitch, always prepared for that vital moment when he alone can keep the ball out. Athletics is now big business, glamorous and global, with the faces of the big name stars featuring on the covers of top-selling magazines. It wasn't good looks that made them sporting superstars, but glamour is seen in a smiling face. I can't remember a television feature on a top runner's toes, yet without toes no one could balance properly, let alone run at world record speeds. Even so in the Church, not every ministry is up front and in the public eye. The back-room jobs, often done so efficiently that they are not even noticed, are just as vital. I think of a retired man who tirelessly greeted people on Sundays and gardened for the elderly throughout the week – Saint Sid has been devoted for many years to unheralded service with a smile.

Paul also stresses three times that every Christian is given at least one gift and some special task in the local fellowship:

'to each one the manifestation of the Spirit is given.' (1 Cor. 12:7)
'God has arranged the parts in the body, every one of them, just as he wanted them to be.' (1 Cor. 12:18)
'Now you are the body of Christ, and each one of you is part of it.' (1 Cor. 12:27)

So much repetition makes it quite clear that Paul is insisting on an essential characteristic of the new community which goes right against the grain of self-interest and conformity to the world. A spiritual gift doesn't belong to me. It is not given for my well-being. It belongs to the Church, and is simply entrusted to me for safekeeping. Every spiritual gift is 'given for the common good' (1 Cor. 12:19–20).

It's not just the gifts that belong to the whole body. Each Christian is part of the body (1 Cor. 12:27) and within the body each has a special function (12:19–20). Because we make up one body, Paul can even say that 'each member belongs to all the others' (Rom. 12:5). As a result, far from looking up to a social élite, or those with a particular gift, all members of the body 'should have equal concern for each other' (1 Cor. 12:25). This is quite shattering for our commuter-style churches, where we sit in our regular places, making our private communion with God, with barely a word for our fellow-worshippers, let alone any strangers. It's not just that we need each other in the sense of needing someone to take the collection, or needing someone to serve the coffee. An isolated Christian, whether refusing to take part in public worship or left on their own in their 'private pew', is, according to the New Testament, a Christian who is incomplete. The community of the Spirit is the place of new belonging. We shouldn't just make each other welcome. We need to discover in practice what it actually means to 'belong to all the others'. Interdependence isn't a mark of inadequacy, it is a hallmark of the body of Christ.

Everyone has something special to give. No one is superfluous. All are different. In fact the Spirit increases our natural diversity, by giving different gifts, to bring us not to clubbish conformity but to the true unity of interdependence. All need to exercise their gifts, and so need opportunities to give. We need to be not just humble enough, but ready and eager to receive from every member. If we don't give, or if we try to give when we don't have the gifts, all suffer. If you don't let someone else give, all miss out. If you desire to do everything, you are quite mistaken. If you think you have nothing to offer, you are just as mistaken. Paul makes it indisputably clear that Christians need each other. To fall out of spiritual dependence on each other is to fall back into old habits of isolation, and to let the world squeeze us back into its mould.

Once given, the gifts need care and effort, because spiritual gifts are not like switching to auto-pilot. Paul was certain that a particular gift had been given to Timothy. But Timothy was naturally shy. A powerful ministry in the public eye went right against his natural temperament. The gift was burning less brightly, and may have been a little neglected, but Paul doesn't doubt it is still present. He urges Timothy to make every effort, in the spirit of 'power, love and self-discipline' (2 Tim. 1:7). He needs to concentrate on the gift God gave and 'fan it into flame' (1:6). We are responsible for the use of the gifts God has given. Sometimes a gift may be given for a particular moment and then withdrawn. But if the decision to withdraw the gift is ours, not the Spirit's, we are playing with fire. Like Timothy, we need to stoke up our spiritual embers, and blaze anew to the glory of God.

Every Christian needs to know what their gifts are, and then put them into practice. That means churches need to provide opportunities for gift identification and implementation. Just as tender shoots need to be protected from the frost, there needs to be a climate of encouragement, so that the first tentative attempts to use a gift won't be crushed, rejected or dismissed. What is more, the availability of spiritual gifts underlines the need for churches to provide clear and varied training programmes. Spiritual gifts are rarely given in a completely mature condition: they need proper development if they are to flourish to the full.

There really is no need for anyone in the Church to feel worthless. Not only did Christ consider each one worth dying for, he has also given every single Christian at least one special gift, often with more on the way. Every single member of the body of Christ is needed. Because no believer has been left out from the distribution of spiritual gifts, every single Christian has an invaluable contribution to make in their local church. The spiritual gifts are provided to strengthen fellowship and create deeper body life as we learn together more about how to both give and receive. It isn't unfortunate that we are all different, it's God's intention. The Church isn't meant to produce pew upon pew of carbon-copy look-alikes, because God's ideal for the Church is a very mixed assortment. This doesn't mean a rag-bag of isolated individuals each doing their own thing. The body of Christ is like a symphony orchestra: only out of many different instruments can a beautiful harmony emerge.

Gifts of leadership

In Ephesians 4 Paul concentrates specifically on leadership gifts, both within and beyond the local church. Five gifts are listed, or more precisely five kinds of leader, each of whom receives appropriate gifting from the Holy Spirit: apostles, prophets, evangelists, pastors and teachers (Eph. 4:11). Once again the only consistent ordering concerns apostles and prophets. Wherever these two gifts are both listed, they always come first.

Three kinds of apostle can be found in the New Testament. First, there is Jesus, the Father's unique 'Apostle'. Whereas for us the term 'apostle' indicates an office and calling of the highest leadership among God's people, in Greek the term literally meant 'a sent one'. Jesus used the equivalent verb when he spoke of being sent from God. An alternative translation for John 20:21 would therefore read: 'As the Father apostled me, I am sending you.' The particular kind of sending that Jesus has in mind is ambassadorial, in which the sent one represents the sender with due authority. Just as he is the eternal Son of God in human flesh, his apostles have the authority and power to represent him in this way because of a critical combination of factors: Jesus calls them and the Holy Spirit fills them.

The foundational eye-witness leaders of the Church are therefore the second kind of apostle, appointed once-for-all by Christ, to provide the decisive leadership and the deposit of permanent authoritative teaching that is the sufficient basis to sustain the Church in every generation. Paul considers himself an addition to the original apostles as one 'untimely born' (1 Cor. 15:8), the special apostle to the Gentiles, called and appointed in an exceptional and emphatic manner as he journeyed towards Damascus intent upon the destruction of the Church. Paul is emphatic that he belongs in the foundational category of apostles, and not in those who have been subsequently appointed to leadership – 'sent by Christ, not men' (Gal. 1:1).

The natural meaning of the term 'apostle' is broader than this foundational group, drawing upon the imprecise nature of the noun in the Greek language. The third category of apostle is therefore the 'sent ones' who have oversight in the wider Church, probably carrying as one of their key tasks a strategic church-planting responsibility, rather than being narrowly focussed on local church ministry. In this broader sense, many others in the New Testament are termed 'apostles', without the unique authority of the foundational apostles being automatically extended to their ministry. We therefore find a significant additional number of leaders referred to as apostles: Barnabas (Acts 14:4, 14;1 Cor. 9:5–6), Silas (1 Thess. 2:6), Titus (2 Cor. 8:23), Epaphroditus (Phil. 2:25), Andronicus and Junias (Rom. 16:7). To make matters more complex for those who insist that leadership is male, just as Deborah was counted among the Judges of Israel, it seems that Junias was almost certainly a woman. The name Junias has a feminine ending in Greek, although it could be an unusual man's name. Early Church and medieval commentators took it for granted that this Junias was a woman, but were men ever called 'Junias'? A little detective work reveals that the name appears 250 times in writings from the time of Paul. Of these, the number of times the name refers to a woman is no less than 250. There is not one example of this name being given to a man. In the early Church it therefore seems likely that this subordinate kind of apostolic ministry was open to women.

Recognising the broad range of meanings that this word carries in Greek, modern translations such as the NIV and the NASB prefer the word 'messenger'. This non-literal approach certainly attempts to clarify the distinction between different kinds of itinerant leader in the early Church. However, this avoidance of the actual term 'apostle' when used with its broader meaning, serves to reinforce the impression that there is no possible validity in the suggestion that there was a continuing apostolic ministry beyond the foundational apostles. The plain grammatical fact in the writings of the New Testament is that the first Christians, including the foundational apostles, were quite relaxed about using the term 'apostle' to describe a wide range of leaders with itinerant ministries. There is therefore no good biblical reason for us being more exclusive, restricting the title to the foundational apostles alone.

This secondary kind of apostleship needs always to be kept carefully distinct from the once-for-all, unique authority and

teaching of the foundational apostles of the first generation. There
is a fundamental difference, and it is vital that the distinction is
never blurred. Of course the role of apostle has sometimes been
fulfilled without the actual title being used. Two of the most
obvious English apostles of previous generations were surely John
Wesley and Charles Spurgeon. In conclusion, there is every reason
to expect, pray for and seek to identify this second kind of apostle
to be raised up in each succeeding generation. We continue to need
leaders with wider than local ministries who carry a particular
church-planting responsibility and are recognised to have particular
spiritual authority, breadth of vision and sharpness of insight. If
the early Church believed in and benefited from this secondary
kind of apostolic ministry, we also need to identify and benefit
from today's apostolic ministries. Without requiring any high
ecclesiastical rank or office, and without any need for ermined robes
or grandiloquent religious titles, such leaders are rightly recognised
as Christ's appointed leaders for the present generation.

Turning to the prophets, these leaders carried a seniority in the
early Church second only to the apostles, usually appearing first
or second in Paul's lists of gifts. New Testament references to the
apostles and prophets have often been taken to refer to the New
and Old Testament writings, despite the fact that much of the Old
Testament is designated by other terms: the Law, the history, wisdom
and poetry. However, when Paul speaks of the Church built upon
the foundation of the apostles and the prophets, it is much more
likely that he is describing the two foundational kinds of leader in
the early Church (Eph. 2:20). We find persuasive evidence for this a
few verses later, when Paul states that things unknown in previous
generations have now been revealed by the Spirit to 'God's holy
apostles and prophets' (3:5). Quite plainly Paul cannot possibly be
referring to the prophets of the Old Testament. The words of these
early Church prophets must have carried considerable weight. In
Acts 13:1, the leadership team in the church at Antioch were not
yet known as elders, but were designated by their particular giftings
as a team comprised of prophets and teachers. Not everyone who
exercised the gift of prophecy was known as a prophet, but only
those whose use of the gift was frequent and carried a particular
authority.

Prophecy comes in many different forms, and the early Church developed a subtle and nuanced approach to recognising prophets and handling their prophesying. The lowest level of prophecy was the occasional prophetic word offered by an individual in the local church. It is in this sense of the word that Paul expressed his desire that every believer might prophesy. The second level was where someone was identified as a prophet, as a result of their regular use of the gift. At the third level, some prophets were appointed to a leadership role in the local church. At a fourth level, some prophets had an itinerant ministry, travelling from church to church. At a fifth level were those prophets whose writings are included in the Old Testament.

This final group are quite distinct in the measure of authority recognised in their words. Their writings alone are preserved as God-breathed Scriptures, unlike the prophecies of the many other Israelite prophets referred to in the Old Testament. This distinction is sustained in the early Church, since, despite the respect attached to ministries of the early Christian prophets, we have no extant collections of the words of an early Church prophet, compiled as a book within the New Testament. The early Church prophets were therefore treated in their prophetic insight as secondary or subservient, compared with the canonical prophets of the Old Testament, just as they were subservient in the authority of their leadership to the New Testament apostles.

We also need to recognise a marked contrast in the treatment of false prophets. Despite the dire warnings of the Old Testament that false prophets should be stoned, there is no report of a single stoning of a false prophet in the early Church. Grace and mercy replace capital punishment. This certainly means that the early Christians were more forgiving, but it also suggests that prophecy was understood in a new way: it was less than ultimate revelation, understood to be subservient to the Scriptures rather than supplementing or replacing them. The early Christians took prophecy seriously enough to promote its continuance with enthusiasm, but they consistently granted it less than the ultimate authority of Scripture.

Pastors, teachers and evangelists are more familiar to many Christians than apostles and prophets. The word 'pastor' signifies a shepherd. Pastoring therefore entails not only caring for the sheep, but also ensuring that they are fed and are growing properly.

Churches' understanding of 'pastor' has often been distorted into someone who drinks lots of cups of tea with people, but biblical pastoring carries clear responsibilities not only of care, but also of vision and leadership. The biblical concept of shepherding cannot be separated from leadership: the true pastor must be concerned to lead the flock forward into the things of God. When Paul gave his farewell address to the Ephesian elders, rather than identifying one of them as 'the pastor', he called them pastors together (Acts 20:28). His primary charge to them was not to provide all the pastoral care, but rather to protect the flock from false teaching (20:29–31).

Paul explained to Timothy that the teacher's great task is to 'correctly handle the Word of Truth' (2 Tim. 2:15). In an age besotted with pluralism and existentialism, many people do what is right in their own eyes, and many believe whatever they happen to feel is true for them. The task of Bible teaching is therefore a high calling and a vital discipline. The Bible teacher must expound the text faithfully and thoroughly, always preferring to declare the Word of the Lord rather than parading his own opinions. Systematic Bible teaching, moving through a particular book chapter by chapter, is an invaluable way of grounding the people of God in the whole counsel of Scripture. Just as the teacher must make space for the prophet, the prophet must respect what may often seem the less spectacular gifts of the teacher. Without a thorough grounding in biblical teaching, the people will be ill-equipped to sift bogus prophecy, whether deceptive or well-intentioned, from the real thing. Pastoring and teaching go hand in hand. Pastors need to ensure that the people are fed with the Word of God. Teachers need a clear understanding of what makes people tick, or their words will lack compassion and sensitivity. Jesus and Paul both had outstanding teaching gifts, one in parables and the other in abstract theology. But their hearers didn't have to climb an ivory tower to understand them. Our teaching, like theirs, must be firmly rooted both in the revealed truth of God in the Scriptures and at the same time in the practical realities of everyday living in today's world.

While all Christians are called to be witnesses, some are gifted to be evangelists. The rest of us cannot legitimately rely on the evangelists to do everything and evade our own task as witnesses to our friends, family and colleagues at work. Nor should evangelists be looked down upon and treated with disdain by other leaders. A welcome development in some denominations and streams in recent years has been a new preparedness to train and recognise evangelists as a separate ministry, rather than lumping everyone together in a monochrome and standardised training for '*the* ministry'. The evangelist has an invaluable reaping ministry: but for his preaching to win converts, others must have been sowing the seed through the double witness of lifestyle and words and by inviting friends to the meeting. There is nothing more soul-destroying for the evangelist than to arrive at an evangelistic meeting to discover that everyone present is a Christian, attending as a form of religious recreation. Just as the Church needs apostles and prophets, pastors and teachers, we also need evangelists. But the effectiveness of their ministry is critically dependent upon every-member witness. Successful reaping by one evangelist requires months of patient and prayerful sowing by many witnesses.

The minister in the body

The Strongest Man in Europe competition has one hugely muscled man dragging along a two-ton truck. Muscles and veins seem fit to burst as the truck inches forward and the seconds tick away. Paul writes of 'every supporting ligament' (Eph. 4:16) and the body 'supported and held together by its ligaments and sinews' (Col. 2:19). His vision is certainly not of some heroic minister, sinews stretched to the limit, dragging behind him a vast, unwieldy, passive congregation.

David Watson warned that the minister is so often the cork in the bottle, holding back the renewal of a local church. I am firmly convinced that, in many churches, the rekindling of body life and the practice of spiritual gifts depend on the leaders stepping aside from the rigid patterns of traditional ministry. Rediscovering the body of Christ can bring great liberation to full-time ministers, but it can also bring great strain. One minister raised the possibility of every-member ministry and was firmly rebuked by his deacons: 'That's what we pay you for!' Another had every-member ministry suggested by his church council and admitted that his gut reaction was: 'But *I've* been trained and ordained to do those things. They are my turf!'

Many ministers have been trained to live as if they were able to meet every need in the local church. The minister alone, or in partnership with fellow full-timers, will make key decisions, lead all the worship, preach every Sunday and do all the official counselling. For an older generation, the need for omnicompetence was quite explicit at theological college. Today it still seeps unspoken into attitudes and ways of seeing 'my ministry'. If someone approaches the minister to suggest that certain lay people may be better at some tasks, it isn't just hackles of pride that may rise. Such comments can seem to threaten a whole ministry. If a person has had it ingrained through a life-time that the minister should be omnicompetent, any suggestion that others may have gifts the minister lacks seems to question the minister's whole calling and even his or her value as a minister. He or she may feel hurt and rejected. Churches need to love ministers out of their isolation and secret vulnerability.

The laity or *laos* is the whole people of God. Full-time ministry is a special calling within the people of God, not a separate and superior caste. Recently I met the new minister at the church where one of our friends has been active for years. 'So you're the new minister at Clive's church,' I said, meaning to be friendly. The reply was a brush-off: 'I prefer to think of Clive as being a member of my church.' The thinking behind 'my church' and 'my people' can set a minister over against ordinary Christians. Ministers can become a world apart, living a 'proper' Christian life in their 'full-time Christian work'. This can lead to clerical snobbery. It also causes 'lay people' to feel that God lets off the rest of us with half-measures of holiness. The New Testament doesn't allow different standards of behaviour before and after entry to full-time ministry. As J.N.D. Kelly, a specialist on the early Church, noted: 'the whole conception of a double standard in basic Christian living was a later intrusion, and represented a falling away from the primitive ideal. All Christians alike . . . were expected to manifest the same spirit . . .' (*Aspects of the Passion*, Mowbray, 1985). John Owen was quite clear that, in the New Testament, gifts of ministry don't 'come with the job', attached automatically to the office of cleric through the rite of ordination. On the contrary, he recognised that leadership gifts come direct from the Spirit – 'The Church has no power to call any person to the office of the ministry, where Christ hath not gone before it in the designation of that person by an endowment of spiritual gifts' (*Pneumatologia*).

Before I entered full-time ministry, we lived for a while in a town where all the ministers swapped churches one Sunday a year, as an expression of Christian unity. I couldn't help but feel that it would have been a much more dramatic expression of unity for all the ministers to stay in their own church, sitting in the congregation while others from each fellowship led the service. For many today, the barriers between denominations are crumbling, but the most sternly guarded frontier is between pulpit and pew. The body of Christ is in peak condition when all its parts are working in harmony, not when one or two full-timers are thoroughly over-worked. Every-member ministry doesn't make the ordained minister redundant. On the contrary, it permits him or her to learn to receive from others in the body and releases them to express their own distinctive God-given gifts of leadership. Perhaps for the first time the minister can really become a leader and member within the body, rather than a partially severed limb. The more the body of Christ is rediscovered, the fuller an individual ministry can be.

Over seventy years ago, an Anglican missionary called Roland Allen wrote an astonishingly prophetic analysis, contrasting modern missionary strategies with the approach of the New Testament. Allen concluded that imperialistic methods produced weak-kneed converts, ever dependent on European missionaries, who held all the reins and remained a priestly race apart. In the last thirty years, his words have finally begun to strike home, not only to missionary societies, but also to patterns of Church life and ministry here in the West:

... the power in which St Paul was able to act with such boldness was the spirit of faith. Faith, not in the natural capabilities of his converts, but in the power of the Holy Ghost in them. Now if we are to practise any methods approaching to the Pauline methods in power and directness, it is absolutely necessary that we should first have this faith, this spirit. Without faith – faith in the Holy Ghost in our converts – we can do nothing. We cannot possibly act as the Apostle acted until we recover this faith. Without it we shall be unable to recognise the grace of the Holy Spirit in our converts, we shall never trust them, we shall never inspire in them confidence in the power of the Holy Spirit in themselves. If we have no faith in the power of the Holy Spirit in them, they will not learn to have faith in the power of the Holy Spirit in themselves. We cannot trust them, and they cannot be worthy of trust; and trust, the trust which begets trustworthiness, is the one essential for any success in the Pauline method. (Roland Allen, *Missionary Methods: St Paul's or Ours?* Eerdmans, 1962)

Interregnum is a wretched word for churches to use, because it is derived from *rex*, the Latin word for king, and Jesus is the only King of his Church; but we know that many churches in an 'interregnum' slip into neutral gear while they await the arrival of the next minister and look forward to the new ministry among them. How much more, according to Paul, do we need to look forward to the release of the gifts of every member, so that the Body of Christ may reach full strength and maturity together.

Gifts for worship

The Corinthians were making a terrible mess of Christian living. However, as Jim Packer warned, this 'must not blind us to the fact that they were enjoying the ministry of the Holy Spirit in a way in which we today are not' (J.I. Packer *Keep in Step with the Spirit*, IVP, 1984). From Paul's letters to the Corinthians we receive not only the words of institution of the Lord's Supper, but also this invaluable description of early Church worship: 'When you come together, everyone has a hymn, or a word of instruction, a revelation, a tongue or an interpretation' (1 Cor. 14:26). Every-member ministry is taken very seriously, not just in theory but in practice. Worship in the Spirit is characterised by rich variety. The living God delights in a combination of prayerful preparation and spontaneous participation.

Paul is uncompromising: 'All of these must be done for the strengthening of the church' (1 Cor. 14:26). On the one hand Paul is emphasising that our motivation must be correct. All must be done for the sake of others. If participation is based on showmanship, the body won't be blessed and the Holy Spirit won't be pleased. At the same time, Paul stresses that for a church to be truly alive in the

Spirit, its worship needs all of these elements. Hymns and instruction, prophecy and tongues, all need the freedom to be present. When all these things are done, to build each other up and not to parade our own gifts, the church is thoroughly strengthened. As C.K. Barrett observed with typical English understatement: 'Church meetings in Corinth can scarcely have suffered from dullness.'

I'm quite sure that Paul should not be taken to mean that the use of every single gift is compulsory at every meeting. But he does insist on the freedom to participate with the full variety of spiritual gifts. We need to make sure that we are applying in our local church this charter of freedom to participate in worship. There is no excuse to brush it under the carpet and pretend it doesn't exist. We have to ask ourselves some searching and maybe uncomfortable questions. Do we pick and choose which gifts will be allowed in our church? Do we decide for ourselves who will be allowed to exercise them? Are these decisions made simply according to our personal taste in worship? If so, are we cramping the freedom of the Spirit to lead our worship and to strengthen our fellowship in the ways he desires?

There are three common objections to this openness. Some object that such worship cannot be orderly: but it is precisely when Paul gives his instruction about orderliness that he provides this description of what our worship should look like. The reality is that the orderliness of human religion is a good deal more predictable, rigid and stuffy than the dynamic orderliness of a meeting conducted under the inspiration of the Holy Spirit. What Paul commends is not the dead order of the graveyard, but a free flow of open worship, steered with a light hand by leaders who are sensitive to the needs of the people, the theme of the preaching and the sudden, creative breath of the Holy Spirit. Others object that open worship is messy, a chaotic free-for-all. The task of worship leaders is not to allow the people to contribute whatever they want, but to help the congregation to learn how to contribute whatever the Holy Spirit wants. Still others object that their fellowship is too large: there's not time for everyone to contribute, and the acoustics of their building mean that often people cannot be heard. Beyond two or three hundred people, the size of a meeting undoubtedly begins to restrict opportunities for open worship. That's no excuse to exclude it, but larger numbers mean an increasing need for front-led worship. There is not only still room for creative openness in these larger meetings, but it also becomes essential for larger churches to promote the use of spiritual gifts and participative worship through smaller meetings, not least in home groups. The spiritual gifts are not optional extras for churches that happen to like that kind of thing. All the gifts are given by the Spirit to build up the body of Christ. The plain teaching of the New Testament is that for the Church to be healthy and strong, all the gifts the Holy Spirit has given need to be in regular use.

RECEIVING AND GIVING

9

New confidence – The Spirit of Love

When our family moved to Sevenoaks in Kent, I was an average sixteen-year-old, eager to live to the full and to be successful at everything. I had never been religious, never been turned on by choirs and candles, but I was increasingly intrigued by Jesus. New friends soon dragged me to Contact, a lively Christian youth group. Contact proved irresistible. Teenagers talked about Jesus as a personal friend and Saviour, their prayers were real and you could see the results. Conversation flowed freely into the small hours about typical mid-teenage concerns – the meaning of life, fair distribution of wealth in the world, and who was going out with whom. What was more, there were plenty of pretty girls!

By early summer I was in a jam. It wasn't girlfriend trouble, and it wasn't an O-level revision crisis. It was Jesus. Most Saturday nights Contact trooped to Hildenborough Hall, the local Christian conference centre. Through films, rock groups and celebrity interviews, the gospel was clearly and consistently presented. Hildenborough was in tune with our needs, reliably imaginative and relevant. There was never any emotional pressure, but if anyone wanted to respond to Christ, they were invited to echo silently a prayer at the end of the meeting. That was my problem. Each week the truth of the gospel became more real. I had made some kind of commitment the previous summer, but everything had remained fairly vague and theoretical. I didn't tell anyone, but each week as they prayed on the platform, I knew afresh my need of Christ. No one else offered promises like his. No one else could take his place. Week after week I echoed that prayer. I wanted to be born again, but how could I be sure anything had really happened? I needed to discover new confidence in Christ's Spirit.

Certain of Christ

Some people hate all certainty. They suggest that being a Christian means being good enough and being religious enough to pass God's entrance exam for heaven. They say that you may hope you are a Christian, but you cannot presume more than that. The apostle Paul once hoped that his life was pleasing to God. He had the finest religious pedigree – born into a good family, circumcised at the right time, a scrupulous Pharisee for every detail of the law, and a zealous persecutor of the Christians (Phil. 3:4–6). But none of this gave him peace with God.

When Paul met the risen Christ on the road to Damascus, his life was transformed. Compared with Christ's free forgiveness, his religious pedigree was worth nothing. Because he turned to Christ, he lost all his old social prestige. A religious pedigree couldn't make Paul confident of God's favour, but in Christ, Paul received the 'righteousness that comes from God and is by faith' (Phil. 3:9). He could never be certain of salvation if it depended on his own goodness, but now he was certain enough to turn from chief persecutor into tireless missionary. His new-found confidence arose not through pride, but through God's free gift of Christ. Paul expresses the heart of the gospel with unforgettable simplicity: '. . . if you confess with your mouth "Jesus is Lord", and believe in your heart that God raised him from the dead you will be saved. For it is with your heart that you believe and are justified, and it is with your mouth that you confess and are saved' (Rom. 10:9–10).

Luther faced the same problem as Paul. He joined a strict order of monks and kept the rules diligently. He did all in his power to put himself right with God. He was desperate for certain forgiveness and drove himself mercilessly in fasting, prayer, reading and other good works. Later he reckoned he would soon have destroyed his health, had he kept it up much longer. Luther understood clearly that all are guilty before God: 'However irreproachable my life as a monk, I felt myself in the presence of God to be a sinner with a most unquiet conscience, nor could I believe him to be appeased by the satisfaction I could offer.' When he realised God's standards, lack of certainty over salvation became an increasing nightmare: 'There can be no flight, nor consolation either from within or from without, but all is accusation.' As Luther studied the New Testament he found the new hope he so desperately needed. Justification cannot be achieved by human efforts since no one can ever make up for their past or fully change themselves for the future. Rather, justification is by faith. Crucified for our sake and risen to bring us new birth, Christ offers salvation with an absolute certainty. Now Luther had a new confidence which his years of determined effort had never won. Now his certainty wasn't rooted in his own achievements, but in Christ and his cross. His discovery of the risen Saviour sparkles with joy – 'At this I felt myself straightaway born afresh and to have entered through the open gates into paradise itself.'

The New Testament promise is clear and consistent. In John's words: 'God has given us eternal life, and this life is in his Son. He who has the Son has life' (1 John 5:11–12). And in Paul's words: 'if anyone is in Christ he is a new creation' (2 Cor. 5:17). The New Testament doesn't leave us on a treadmill of uncertainty. We don't have to keep trying to prove we are good enough for God. The true certainty of the gospel is centred on Christ alone. This isn't misplaced pride or presumption. When we receive Christ, we receive the love that won't ever let us down: '. . . we have been made holy through the sacrifice of the body of Jesus Christ once for all' (Heb. 10:10).

Life in fragments

Tom Stoppard's play, *Rosencrantz and Guildenstern are Dead* is an extremely funny parable of modern men and women's lostness. These two very ordinary people with extraordinary names keep bumping into characters from Shakespeare's Hamlet, who speak in Elizabethan poetry from the quill of the bard and give orders to our two heroes. They just don't belong in this strange world, but it controls them, and even arranges their deaths. Life doesn't fit into any kind of intelligible and coherent order but they are helpless to change it.

Jean-Paul Sartre looked at the way people can destroy each other and concluded, '*L'enfer, c'est les autres*' – Hell is other people. He said that conventional fiction is a reassuring lie, because it provides a beginning, middle and end. According to Sartre, novels assert that life has a shape, order and meaning, which is what we all long for. But real life is a series of chance collisions, an accident without a purpose.

The Old Testament is no stranger to this theme of alienation. The first eleven chapters of Genesis show sin to be its source. The first act of disobedience leads quickly to evasion of responsibility. Adam tries to persuade God it was 'all *her* fault'. Man is sentenced to sweat and toil: work becomes an unfortunate and often unenjoyable necessity. A new conflict arises between humans and nature. 'Cursed is the ground because of you; through painful toil you will eat of it all the days of your life. It will produce thorns and thistles for you' (Gen. 3:17–18). Soon the first murder happens, and like the majority of murders ever since it is within the family. After that there develops an explosive increase of lust, idolatry, pride and irreligion. Sin isn't a one-off. It multiplies faster than rabbits.

Paul explores four different dimensions of this alienation that finds its ultimate source in the fall. Together these four aspects express the profound dissatisfaction that is often expressed in modern art and that underlies the universal human quest for meaning and fulfilment.

(i) We are cut off from God
Many express an aching need for God that nothing else can satisfy, because we have been created for relationship with God. But actions and attitudes often go against that need. People are alienated from God, being his 'enemies in their minds' (Col. 1:21). Books that attack Jesus make headlines. Call him a myth or a mushroom, or say a double was crucified while Jesus escaped with Mary Magdalene to France – any nonsense will do – and you have a best-seller. There is an instinctive antipathy in society to Jesus and his followers.

(ii) We are cut off from nature
The pollution and destruction of natural resources is a terrible legacy of the industrial age. But alienation goes deeper than that, for nature is subjected to frustration and disorder by human beings

who are alienated from it (Rom. 8:19–23). I love fell-walking. Within minutes you can be alone with nature. Around you is spectacular beauty; freshly-shooted grass clambers over unconquerable volcanic rock, ages old. Yet even as the glorious beauty quickens your pulse and fills you with delight and praise, a curious feeling of alienation can arise. Wordsworth was never more at home than when walking in the Lake District. His poetry will last for as long as poetry is read. Yet not even Wordsworth ever felt fully at home, because we don't quite belong in nature any more.

> Waters on a starry night
> Are beautiful and fair;
> The sunshine is a glorious birth:
> But yet I know, where'er I go,
> That there hath passed away a glory from the earth.
>
> (*Ode: Intimations of Immortality*)

(iii) We are cut off from each other

You don't need to teach children selfishness, it is there from birth. 'Mine' and 'want it' soon turn into shoving other children away from their toys. Through race and class and caste, through insult and inability to trust, we cut ourselves off from each other. The 'works of the flesh' are a catalogue of our mutual hostility and antagonism. But in our heart of hearts we don't want it that way. An American soldier in Vietnam killed an enemy guerrilla with a knife, but then said, 'I felt sorry. I don't know why I felt sorry. John Wayne never felt sorry.' While the divorce rate rises faster and faster, men and women still long for loving relationships that last.

(iv) We are cut off from ourselves

In Romans chapter 7 Paul describes inner or self-alienation. Life is made up of contradictory fragments. We cannot see clearly an overall pattern. Left to ourselves we have no adequate chart for self-reconstruction. God's law shows how life can be lived – loving God with all we've got and loving our neighbours as ourselves. Those who try hardest to fulfil God's commands conclude that it is simply not possible without Christ. The more we look inside, the more we discover the power of the sinful nature. For John Donne, this inner conflict became almost unbearable: 'O to vex me, contraries meet in one.'

Only in Jesus do we see the human wholeness, integration and harmony intended by God. Only through Jesus can that deepest wholeness begin to be recovered. For it was Jesus who promised: 'I have come that you might have life, and have it abundantly' (John 10:10). This wholeness and abundant life depend on living encounters with the love of God. Paul sums up this kind of glorious experience of the love of God that can overwhelm alienation and distress in life: 'Hope does not disappoint us, because God has poured out his love into our hearts by the Holy Spirit, whom he has given us' (Rom. 5:5).

Beginning in the Spirit

The New Testament writers are fully confident that Christ's atoning sacrifice has paid the price of sin once for all. But a bridge still has to be built from a doctrine on paper to a belief in the heart. The general statement that Christ died for sinners needs to become a personal conviction that Christ died for me. Jesus must come to be seen not merely as a distant controller of the cosmos, but as Lord of my life. This turns biblical ideas into saving faith, where head theory becomes heart commitment. That's where the Spirit is so crucial. Only by the Spirit can anyone claim Jesus as Saviour. In fact, Jesus explains that he begins work even earlier, for the Spirit 'convicts the world' of sin (John 16:8). Without the Spirit, none of us could even be converted in the first place.

This is why Paul is so direct in his letter to the Romans: 'If anyone does not have the Spirit of Christ, he does not belong to Christ' (Rom. 8:9). Paul doesn't say this to provoke agonised soul-searching among the Roman converts as to whether they have the Spirit. He simply will not allow a rigid line to be drawn between receiving Christ and receiving the Spirit. It is by the 'Spirit of Christ' that Christ is received. Paul has no time for the suggestion that receiving the Spirit is actually meant to be a separate and later experience, to upgrade the believer beyond new life in Christ. Only in the Spirit is the new life possible, and where there is a living confession of Christ as Lord, there is the Spirit. We have to be equally careful of the opposite overstatement. Paul doesn't say, 'I received the Spirit at conversion, so I don't want to talk about him any more.' He nowhere suggests that conversion is the sum and the end of the Spirit's activity in the believer. But conversion is quite unmistakably where life in the Spirit is meant to begin.

Paul's understanding of the Spirit is penetrating and profound, and his teaching on the spirit is invaluable and practical for every believer and every fellowship. None of it was written just for academics to theorise over. The Spirit himself breathes through the words of the Bible with unfailing relevance, and at every moment the Spirit's impact is centred on Christ, because the Spirit always glorifies Jesus and helps us to be responsive to him.

Spirit of assurance

The most important passage Paul wrote on assurance is Romans 8:9–27. In a few sentences he raises many key ways in which the Spirit provides new confidence. These principles are not meant for theoretical analysis alone. The Spirit comes to write them on every believer's heart.

(i) God with me
'His Spirit lives in you' (Rom. 8:11). One of the names given to Jesus was 'Immanuel', which means 'God with us' – a clear indication that God was breaking into human history in a new way. Our salvation has been made complete already, in Christ's cross and resurrection, but that doesn't mean that God then removed himself to a remote distance from humankind. The objective cross in history is the unshakeable foundation for my present confidence before God, and the Holy Spirit bridges the two-thousand-year gap between the cross and life today. The Spirit makes Christ's death personal to each Christian. He makes the Bible come alive. His presence confirms that when Christ died, my salvation was won. It is by his Spirit that Jesus now continues to be available as 'God with us'.

(ii) The prayer of Jesus
'By the Spirit we cry, "*Abba*, Father"' (Rom. 8:15). I was waiting to check in at Tel Aviv airport when a little child rushed up to his

Father. '*Abba, abba!*' was his eager and noisy cry, as he expressed his delight that his daddy had come home. Until the time of Jesus, no Jew had ever dared to use this intimate childhood word as a way of addressing God. Many must have been horrified by Jesus's deliberate choice of the word '*Abba*'. Yahweh was so holy, so awesome, that some insisted that his name could not even be written down or spoken. Jesus breaks with all traditional reverence by calling God '*Abba*'. Said frivolously, such a way of addressing God would be close to blasphemy. What Jesus reveals is a unique confidence in God's love, and a unique closeness to him as Father.

This prayer had an enormous impact on the first Christians. It is quoted twice by Paul in the original Aramaic, when writing to Greek-speaking Christians (Rom. 8:15; Gal. 4:6). It seems clear that the actual word of Jesus was used both in public and private prayer – 'the Spirit who calls out, "*Abba*, Father"' (Gal. 4:6). The word for a new kind of prayer crossed language barriers along with the gospel. Only Jesus could call God '*Abba*' by right. Because Jesus has paid the price for human sin, his followers could dare to enter into Jesus's intimate relationship with God. In the one Spirit, all could pray to the Father with a new intimacy expressed in the prayer of the Son.

We have lost the shock of calling God '*Abba*' and also the implications of a radical intimacy with the Father. Habit can stifle intimacy and so it has become possible to pray to God as 'Father', and yet relate to him in very formal and distant terms. The Spirit wants to draw us back into Jesus's closeness to God. This doesn't mean we model our relationship with God on our relationship with our earthly father. It is Jesus alone who shows us what God the Father is like, and how to relate to him. The Spirit of Jesus didn't come just to enhance prayer, he came to transform it. God isn't simply with us, nor simply our Saviour, wonderful as those truths about him are. He is *Abba*, our 'dear father', and even our 'heavenly dad'.

(iii) Spirit of adoption
'Those who are led by the Spirit of God are sons of God' (Rom. 8:14). Some speak as if all people are God's children by birthright, but in the New Testament God has only one Son. Without Christ, humans are not sons of God but rather 'slaves to fear', because we

have no confidence before God. It is therefore a further indication of our new status in Christ that the Holy Spirit is called the Spirit of 'adoption' and of 'sonship'. *Adoption* under Roman law brought equal rights with natural children. Our adopted status therefore grants us the unreserved and permanently secure condition of full children of God. *Sonship* indicates equality with Christ. In Christ we become co-heirs. The promise naturally does not apply only to men. Nor does it imply that men are in any sense superior to women in Christ. What Paul indicates in the shorthand idiom of his age is that all believers are made sons, which means that all are equal, all are adopted, and all are co-heirs with Christ. Once we recognise the full equality of the sexes, we can then translate Paul's meaning as the Spirit of adoption for daughters and for sons alike.

Where the Spirit is, there is adoption. We don't just call God *'Abba'*, we receive the privileges and responsibilities of becoming God's children. In Christ God was reconciling the world to himself, and so in the Church the ministry of reconciliation must be continued (2 Cor. 5:18–19). To be co-heirs with Christ means that we will share in the unsearchable riches of Christ's glory, but it also means that we may share in his sufferings, rejected like our Master (Phil. 1:29).

(iv) Spirit of inner testimony

'The Spirit testifies with our spirit that we are God's children' (Rom. 8:16). For many Christians, God remains a celestial policeman. Guilt is the dominant mark of the relationship. He seems to tower over you, ready to clap you in irons and punish you for every minor offence. Failure and apology dog your tracks. In prayer you begin to feel like the naughty child who can't look his parents straight in the eye. To be sure, the Spirit convicts us of sin, but he also assures us of forgiveness. Satan, however, merely condemns, accusing us as an end in itself. He seeks to crush Christians with a sense of guilt and failure. He is heard in cries of self-rejection – 'I'm useless.' 'There's no way out.' 'I despair of myself.' His accusations are essentially and deliberately destructive.

Conviction by the Spirit is essentially and deliberately positive. The Spirit exposes our sin in order to point us to Jesus as Saviour. He convicts us for forgiveness and for deliverance. Spirit-inspired confession is filled with love and hope, as guilt is replaced by confidence in Christ. Wesley wrote of boldly approaching the eternal throne, and that vibrant assurance can be granted by the Spirit. Faced with our doubts and weaknesses, the Spirit still points to Jesus. He speaks in quiet and sensitive ways when we feel inadequate or undeserving of God's love. Should the pressures of modern life stretch us to breaking point, and should our minds whirl with the demands of work or family, with problem relationships or unpaid bills, the Holy Spirit continues to be with us, assuring us of God's love.

Through inner stillness the voice of assurance speaks, when we hear a whisper in our hearts that we are truly children of God. God knows that we need this inner testimony, but it is elusive when our lives are too busy and when we live in a turmoil of noise. Music, children, television and machinery surround us with sound. Anxiety or ceaseless brainstorming can make a cacophony of noise within. I once knew someone whose eyes glazed over after ten minutes of any conversation. It wasn't that he was asleep: he simply couldn't keep his mind off his work for longer than that. We need to learn again to hear the Spirit's voice on the inside, speaking to our hearts the promises of Scripture. He tells us we are God's adopted children, in countless different but always appropriate ways. We need to help each other to hear the Spirit's testimony and to drink deep of the love of God.

Imagine Peter and his dad out walking. Peter is young and enjoys holding his father's hand, pleased that the two of them are enjoying time together. Suddenly, and without warning, the father swings Peter up into the air, grinning as he holds him above his head. Peter yells out with delight at this unexpected fun. When they were walking hand in hand, he knew that he was loved, but when his father swirled him off the ground he experienced being loved in a moment of pure pleasure. It was one of the Puritan leaders, so often caricatured as kill-joys and religious miseries, who used this glorious picture of innocent family fun to illustrate what it means to experience the inner testimony of the Spirit. By faith we already know that we are the adopted children of God, holding on to the promises of Scripture that apply to everyone who puts their trust in Christ. But when the Spirit's testimony is experienced within, then we know on the inside that we really are loved by God. This inner witness to the intensity and immensity of our heavenly Father's love is the highest, the most exquisite and powerful form of

Christian assurance. Small wonder that when Whitefield, Edwards and others taught about this witness of the Spirit during the Great Awakening, some would cry out, overwhelmed with joy, 'He has come! He has come!'

(v) Teaches how to pray

'. . . the Spirit helps us in our weakness. We do not know what we ought to pray for' (Rom. 8:26). For a while young children can become devoted to one phrase – 'Mummy, I want . . .! Daddy, I want . . .' A relationship is measured in more than demands. Even so, prayer is much more than petitions – the Lord's Prayer is half said before the first request is made. In Romans 8, Paul reveals a further dimension of prayer. The Spirit prays for Christians (8:27) even as Christ prays for us in heaven (8:34). Such is perfect prayer, in total accordance with the Father's will.

The same Spirit also prays within us aligning our prayers with his own prayers and the prayers of Christ. Words are stretched to the limit in Paul's most daring description of Spirit-led prayer: 'the Spirit himself intercedes for us with groans that words cannot express' (Rom. 8:26). The Spirit draws us into communion with the inner harmony of the Trinity. In the Spirit, our prayer enters into something of the perfect will and perfect love of God. This description of prayer beyond words helps us to understand the gift of tongues. But this is about more than tongues. To hear someone groaning in an agony of prayer can sound very disturbing, but Paul says that some prayers that the Spirit inspires are beyond the limits of expression in human language. Often such depths of prayer express a longing for revival and a grief at how distant our society has become from the ways of our holy God.

(vi) Power to raise

'He who raised Christ from the dead will also give life to your mortal bodies through his Spirit' (Rom. 8:11). We have seen how the Spirit writes on each converted heart, 'Christ was crucified for me.' The certainty of Christ's past sacrifice gives us present confidence that we are saved. But Christ didn't stay dead: God's power raised him, and now God's power lives in us. That means that the resurrection of the first Easter was not a one-off. We don't have fingers crossed in a vague and tentative hope of some kind of survival after death.

The Spirit's power in our lives today provides faith for the future. His presence confirms that just as Jesus was raised, we will be raised. He provides lasting confidence that we are heading for heaven.

(vii) Guarantee to raise
'We . . . have the firstfruits of the Spirit' (Rom. 8:23). The power of God means that we can be raised. The promise of God is that he will do it. When the first fruit appears in my garden, the harvest is not far behind. I'm always eager to taste the first fruit. Its quality gives a foretaste of the coming harvest. The glorious riches of the Spirit are God's first fruit for his children. Our boldest dreams cannot imagine the lavish and inexhaustible riches of the harvest in heaven. God's love is extravagant beyond human measure. In the words of the song, we 'ain't seen nothin' yet!'

Paul talks about the Spirit's promise of resurrection in two more ways: as a seal and as a deposit. A merchant used to stamp his seal on goods he had bought, indicating that he would come to claim them later. 'God . . . set his seal of ownership on us' (2 Cor. 1:22). 'You were marked in him with a seal, the promised Holy Spirit' (Eph. 1: 13). The Spirit is the stamp of God's ownership, assuring us of his love, confirming his lordship, and setting us apart. He is the seal of promise because he fulfils both Old Testament prophecies and the promises of Jesus, but also because his presence is a guarantee that Jesus will come again. The experience of the seal of the Spirit is designed to be understood as a declaration and demonstration that Jesus really is returning to claim us as his own.

The Spirit is also 'a deposit, guaranteeing what is to come' (2 Cor. 1:22; 5:5). He is God's down-payment, 'guaranteeing our inheritance until the redemption of those who are God's possession' (Eph. 1:14). Our present experiences of the Spirit confirm that heaven is ahead. We have the down-payment, and he guarantees that far more will follow. In modern Greek, the word Paul uses for 'deposit' – *arrabon* – has taken on the meaning of an engagement ring. The Spirit is the engagement ring for the Church, the Bride of Christ, guaranteeing the glorious marriage of all eternity.

(viii) Yearning for fulfilment
'We . . . groan inwardly as we wait eagerly for our adoption as sons, the redemption of our bodies' (Rom. 8:23). To desire something more

from life and to aspire to personal growth and development is natural and healthy. As J. S. Mill observed, 'Rather a dissatisfied man than a satisfied pig.' For the Christian, a new era has dawned, but present experience is in the overlap. Life has been set on a new footing. The final transformation is certain and will be greater still. The foretaste we now enjoy prepares us for all that is 'not yet'. We already have the Spirit of adoption, yet the final separation from sin and decay is still to come. Salvation has three tenses: our salvation was completed at the cross; we are saved on confession of faith; but not till beyond death or the return of Jesus Christ will our salvation be fulfilled. The Spirit is given for this life, and he is provided to help us in our everyday living, not for religious escapism. He never makes us super-spiritual: too heavenly-minded to be any earthly use. But the Spirit does make us yearn for the coming fulfilment. He makes us hungry for heaven.

Confident in the Spirit

Paul gets thoroughly excited about the Spirit. He breathes new confidence into believers in so many different ways. There is one vital fact we must emphasise in conclusion. The Spirit isn't a theory on paper or an impersonal power; we are meant to know him in experience. Most of us are very cautious about this. More than forty years ago Lesslie Newbigin warned: 'Theologians today are afraid of the word "experience" . . . the New Testament writers are free from this fear. They regard the gift of the Holy Spirit as an event which can be unmistakably recognised' (*The Household of God*, 1955).

The Galatian church began to think of salvation as a reward, merited if you did enough good. To Paul this was disastrous. The Spirit is the Spirit of grace. He is given through Christ. If the Galatians went back to legalism, they would turn their backs on Christ, and forfeit his Spirit. Paul clinches his argument with a question about their spiritual experience: 'I would like to learn just one thing from you: Did you receive the Spirit by observing the law, or by believing what you heard?' (Gal. 3:2).

We need to seek God, not experience of God. The Spirit draws attention to Christ, not to himself. 'I looked to the Son of God and the dove of peace flew into my heart. I looked to the dove of peace, but he had flown.' Experience is not the Christian's first priority, but that cannot take away the confidence with which Paul questions the Galatians. He is quite certain that the Spirit will have made his presence felt. Some Christians want to explain it all away – 'Must have been caused by strong coffee or all those modern songs!' So often experience of the Spirit is stifled as if all experience is at best dangerous and at worst deranged, but Paul was consistently confident that the Spirit makes his presence felt.

If we are to be truly evangelical, we must rediscover the first Christians' openness to God. If we desire their unrestrained confidence in Christ, we need to receive it through the Spirit, illumining Scripture and kindling in our hearts a living flame of love. Paul expected a confident answer from every Christian to the question: 'Have you received the Spirit?' He expected it not from pure theory, but from living experience. The Spirit hasn't changed. He can be experienced in the same ways today. He can still provide all the assurance that made Paul so excited. We need to learn again how to be always receptive, always open to his glorious presence. Whitefield spoke of this experience of the Spirit as the 'felt Christ'. He encouraged people not only to give intellectual assent to the truths of the gospel, nor only to repent for their sins, but to persistently seek for this encounter with divine assurance. In the same way, it is a glorious sight to see the Spirit of God poured out mightily upon meetings today with many Christians drinking deeply of holy and everlasting love.

The heartbeat of love

New leaves seem to be a miracle each spring. A few weeks before, so many plants seemed dead. Until the earth grows warm again, the plant's life withdraws deep inside. But for new buds to break out, that life must already be within. It's not much help talking about life's problems if there is no way forward. If we want to become confident Christians, we have to begin with the love of God. We need to see ourselves in resurrection light. Sin and death are already defeated. Our lives may be in fragments, but God has already acted. New wholeness can grow because God's love comes to us by the Spirit. John tells us time and again that God is love. We know God's love because he sent Jesus to die for us. We love

God because he first loved us. John keeps spelling it out because
it takes time to sink in.

Jesus recognised the same problem. He taught very clearly how
much God loves us, but his words are so astonishing that we tend
to either misread them or play them down – 'You have loved them
even as you have loved me' (John 17:23). Jesus insists that God
really loves us:

> As much as we deserve?
> Far more.
> As much as anything he created?
> Even more.
> How much, then?
> As much as he loves Jesus.

If Jesus hadn't taught it, no other Christian would dare to suggest
it. Jesus is God's only Son. Jesus shares in the perfect love of the
Trinity. Jesus delights in the will of the Father, and never rejected
him through sin. But God loves each one of us as much as he
loves Jesus.

> . . . be absolutely certain that our Lord loves you, devotedly,
> and individually: loves you just as you are. How often that
> conviction is lacking even in those souls who are most
> devoted to God! They make repeated efforts to love him,
> they experience the joy of loving, and yet how little they know,
> how little they realise, that God loves them incomparably more
> than they will ever know how to love him. Think only of this
> and say to yourself, 'I am loved by God more than I can either
> conceive or understand!' Let this fill all your soul and all your
> prayer and never leave you. (Abbé de Tourville, *Letters of
> Spiritual Direction*, Mowbray, 1982)

This is the spark of life in the heart of darkness. This is the
certain hope that makes wholeness more than a fanciful dream.
In all our failings, weakness and self-contradiction, God loves us.
He has not only made forgiveness secure. He makes a new inner
harmony possible. The heartbeat of wholeness is the life-giving love
of God. Only the Spirit can make this real on the inside. Only by

the Spirit dare we say, 'God truly loves me as much as he loves Jesus!' Only when the sap of the Spirit is flowing freely can a new inner harmony begin to bloom, confident in the love of God which is ours in Christ.

At a recent celebration where I was preaching, a new convert was among those who came forward asking for prayer. She explained that she had only been a Christian for two-and-a-half weeks and had previously been a Muslim.

'What do I need to do when I'm prayed for?' she asked.

'Just be centred on Jesus and be ready to receive,' I explained, and then laid hands upon her and prayed that Jesus would fill her with the Holy Spirit. With a sudden cry of joy she sank to the ground, overcome by the presence of God, and I left her there resting in her Saviour's presence.

Later I heard her talking with some friends: 'It's really wonderful,' she enthused. 'I could feel the love of Jesus flowing right into me.'

In all her years as a Muslim, she believed in Allah and feared her God. But only when she was filled with the Holy Spirit could she know the love of God in her inmost being. Only by the Spirit can we know the love of heaven to earth come down.

Paul prayed in his letter to the Ephesians that with our minds we would grasp as fully as possible the enormity of the love of God: 'I pray that you, being rooted and established in love, may have power, together with all the saints, to grasp how wide and long and high and deep is the love of Christ, and to know this love that surpasses knowledge – that you may be filled to the measure of all the fullness of God.' (Eph. 3:17–19). There is nothing anti-intellectual about God's love. On the contrary, there is no higher object of contemplation for the human mind than the extravagance of divine mercy found in the cross of Christ. At the same time, Paul prayed for a heart-level response to God's love – that we would enjoy living encounters with this love. Paul does not believe for one moment that our capacity to experience God's love is limited by the size of our brain. Rather, he prays that, irrespective of our brainpower, our encounters with God's love will richly transcend our understanding.

Still Paul's prayer is not complete. He has prayed for our minds to be stretched and our hearts to be warmed, and then he prays that we will be filled to the overflow. At a petrol garage there is nothing more frustrating than a pump that keeps flowing when your tank is full, giving your feet a sudden soaking if you don't step hurriedly out of the way. Paul doesn't pray that we will be filled to our capacity with the love of God. Instead he prays that the measure of our filling will be the enormity of God's love – 'filled to the measure of all the fullness of God'. What this means is that God has the capacity to lavish so much love upon us that we not only know and delight in the truth that we are loved in Christ, but more than that, the love of Christ can begin to well up within us and flow freely to those around us and back to our God of love. May we know what it is to live in this overflowing abundance as the Holy Spirit floods us repeatedly with the love of Christ!

10

New Boldness – The Spirit of Evangelism

In this chapter we shall explore Luke's account of how the Spirit brings new boldness in evangelism. But in order to understand the Spirit's role in evangelism clearly, we need first to spell out the exclusivity of the Christian gospel. The Old Testament revealed that God's Spirit is the ultimate source of all life and creativity. But the New Testament insists that the personal and permanent presence of the Spirit is only possible through Christ. The first Christians were convinced that they alone had entered the new age of the Spirit. They had been faithful Jews, but this new experience of God went way beyond anything they had known before. This isn't an arrogant claim that because they are such good people, they have earned the right for God to fill them with his Spirit. They make no pretence to be any better than anyone else in themselves. Their settled conviction is that because Jesus is the Giver of the Spirit, only those who come to Jesus for forgiveness and a fresh start can possibly experience new life in the Spirit: 'Salvation is found in no one else, for there is no other name under heaven given to men by which we must be saved' (Acts 4:12).

It's not that the Church is in control of the Spirit. Rather, the Church can only be Christ's Church when he pours out his Spirit in spiritual rebirth. Many people don't like these exclusive claims. They want all religions and all good people to be inspired in exactly the same way. There is no room for this in the New Testament. The first Christians were exclusive about the Spirit because they were exclusive about Jesus Christ. Only through Jesus, salvation. Therefore only through Jesus, the gift of the Spirit. This exclusivity was summed up by Jesus himself, when he taught about the Spirit: 'The world cannot accept him, because it neither sees him nor knows him' (John 14:17).

A great chasm is fixed between the world and Jesus's followers. No one crosses the chasm by right of birth or by natural goodness. Jesus's followers aren't better people, they are simply those who have already accepted forgiveness on God's terms. Our responsibility to the world is immense: in our lives and words we carry the offer of salvation. In the words of Rebecca Manley Pippert, 'The first Bible many people read will be your life' (*Out of the Saltshaker*, IVP, 1980).

Who's in charge here?

There's nothing wrong with planning and strategy, so long as God isn't left out until the last minute, and then invited to bless our bright ideas. Jesus wanted the Spirit to be in charge, and so the disciples had to sit and wait in Jerusalem until he came in power. When he arrived he certainly made his presence felt. The disciples might not have planned it that way, but their very first taste of the Spirit thrust them into the public eye. Almost before they knew it, they were into mass evangelism. Before follow-up or nurture groups were invented, there were three thousand Christians, and this was their first day of life in the Spirit. No wonder Jesus had told them to wait.

Jesus directed the disciples to reach out in ever greater circles: 'in Jerusalem, and in all Judea and Samaria, and to the ends of the earth' (Acts 1:8). Luke records that, step by step, the Church fulfilled Jesus's command. First the gospel is proclaimed in Jerusalem, where numbers rose swiftly from three thousand to over five thousand (1:1–7:60). It spread through Palestine and Samaria (8:1–9:31) and then it reached the first Gentiles and Antioch (9:32–12:24). The second half of Acts records the spread of the gospel through Asia Minor (12:25–16:5), Europe (16:6–19:20) and finally to Rome (19:21–28:31). Across the known world followers of The Way were baptised into Christ and the Church continued to grow in the power of the Spirit.

Pentecost is not only the birth of the Church, but also represents a kind of preview, anticipating the unfolding story of mission to the world. Jews from many countries are gathered in Jerusalem for the festival. Later in Acts the gift of tongues will be used in worship without being overheard by outsiders. But at the beginning, all hear the mighty acts of God, declared 'in our own tongues' (2:11). Those who suggest that the disciples were simply speaking very clearly or very loudly deserve a special award for text evasion: if you don't like it, at all costs explain it away! The judgment upon Babel is reversed. There, city dwellers with a common language reached up to God in an absurd expression of human pride: a kind of prehistoric Manhattan to the ultimate degree (Gen 11:1–9). Now in Jerusalem, visitors with many different native languages were all spoken to through this first expression of the miraculous gift of tongues. The glorious gospel of Christ, in the power of the Spirit, has the power to unite again the divided peoples of the earth. The task of the newborn Church is to witness to everyone, because Jesus is for all mankind.

Spirit of surprises

The Spirit doesn't just bring results, he brings surprises. If ever the Spirit is in charge, Christians can expect the unexpected and guarantee the unpredictable. When Philip evangelises the Samaritans, everything follows the familiar pattern. They express new-found repentance and faith in Christ. They are baptised, but something is missing: the Spirit doesn't make his presence felt. Only when apostles arrive from the Jerusalem headquarters are the problems ironed out. Not until then are the Samaritan conversions completed, when they 'received the Holy Spirit' (Acts 8:17).

Endless ink has been spilt over this event. Some say the Spirit is given to the Church, and can only be passed on through hands in the apostolic succession. That makes Acts 8 the first confirmation service. Others say that the presence of the apostles is incidental, and the key element is receiving the Spirit as a normative second blessing. Not surprisingly, the majority of commentators feel both these interpretations push the evidence too far. If either was correct, all the other events in Acts would need to be leant on extremely hard in order to try to make them fit this pattern. The Samaritan Pentecost is certainly not best explained by either the rite of confirmation or a mandatory second blessing. Most interpreters look instead to the ancient division between the Jews and the Samaritans. Both claimed to worship Yahweh, but as separate nations, with separate temples and priesthoods. Crossing into Samaria was the first critical expansion of the Christian Church. Would the believers retain their new-found unity in Christ, or would they divide along the old national lines?

The Samaritans could have decided they were as much Christians as the converted (or Messianic) Jews. They could have set up the Samaritan Christian denomination. According to long-established prejudices and mutual mistrust, this was not just possible but highly likely. We can therefore conclude that the Lord deliberately withheld the Spirit because an unexpected but crucial lesson had to be learned. For the Samaritans, it was the unmistakable discovery that they were part of the one new Church of Christ. They could not hang on to national independence and go it alone. For the Jews, on the authority of the apostolic eyewitness reports of both Peter and John, the Samaritans had come into the same experience of the Spirit. Jews could no longer claim national superiority, for all were equal in the one new people of God.

The next major advance in mission got even Peter into trouble (Acts 10). He had been praying and fasting when he fell into a trance and saw a vision. Peter knew quite clearly that some things were unclean, and it took the same vision three times over to prepare him for a triple shock:

> He saw heaven opened and something like a large sheet being let down to earth by its four corners. It contained all kinds of four-footed animals, as well as reptiles of the earth and birds of the air. Then a voice told him, 'Get up, Peter. Kill and eat.' 'Surely not, Lord!' Peter replied. 'I have never eaten anything impure or unclean.' The voice spoke to him a second time, 'Do not call anything impure that God has made clean.' This happened three times, and immediately the sheet was taken back to heaven. (Acts 10:11–16)

The surprises came thick and fast. First Peter was invited to the house of the centurion Cornelius, who was not only a Gentile, he was also a senior figure in the occupying army: a centurion in the Italian Regiment. Second, when he got there they asked for a sermon. Third, he had barely warmed to his theme when his hearers began to speak loudly. This wasn't Gentile rudeness; they were praising God with the gift of tongues. Peter's vision had prepared him, and his sermon had explained the principle that God has no favourites among the nations, but Peter and those with him were still astonished. The Spirit hadn't even waited for him to finish before bringing new life to the Gentiles: 'Then Peter said, "Can anyone keep these people from being baptised with water? They have received the Holy Spirit just as we have"' (10:46-7).

Predictably, some Jewish Christians were up in arms when the news got back to Jerusalem. As soon as possible they called a meeting and criticised Peter for so much as entering Cornelius' house and sharing a meal with Gentiles. Poor Peter was on the defensive. The ex-champion of ritual purity had to defend treating Gentiles as equals. He was careful to show it wasn't his idea. It was the Lord who spoke to him in a vision, and the Spirit who told him to go without delay. Before Peter had even considered baptising the Gentiles, the Spirit had chosen to come upon them, 'as at the beginning' (11:8, 12, 15).

Later, when the Church had to decide whether Jewish law should apply to Gentile Christians, Peter recalled the unexpected events at Cornelius' house: 'God, who knows the heart, showed that he accepted them by giving the Holy Spirit to them, just as he did to us. He made no distinction between us and them, for he purified their hearts by faith' (15:8-9). The Spirit's coming on Cornelius had made an unforgettable impression, demonstrating that God's plan was bigger than Jewish purity. The disciples had been slow to understand Jesus before his crucifixion. Even now the impact of the Great Commission was only just dawning. The gospel is relevant to everyone, and Jesus's promises are equally available to people of all nations. There would be no outer courts for Gentiles and inner courts for Jews in the new age. If you are a Gentile reading this, be thankful. It is only because of the power of the Spirit that we are full members of the Christian Church. And if you are a Jewish Christian, it is because of the Spirit that we share in Christ that you can treat us not as inferiors, but equals, in the new Israel. The barriers of national pride and division have been decisively blown apart.

The Spirit was in charge, and the Spirit spurred the Church into evangelism. Being a Christian and bearing witness to Christ became inseparable. What was more, the Spirit was always unpredictable, coming in power and breathing new life wherever he wanted, not where men had planned. When it comes to fulfilling Jesus's promises, the Spirit was and has always continued to be several steps ahead of the Church. Christian witness is not an occasional obligation for enthusiasts, but the instinctive, normal and continual mark of the presence of the Spirit. To attempt to evangelise without the Spirit was expressly discouraged by Jesus. To claim the Spirit for 'my' experience, and leave evangelism to others was, for the first Christians, unthinkable nonsense.

When J. B. Phillips translated the book of Acts, he discovered in these pages 'the fresh air of heaven plainly blowing':

> The Spirit of God found what surely he must always be seeking – a fellowship of men and women so united in love and faith that he can work in them and through them with the minimum of let and hindrance. Consequently it is a matter of sober historical fact that never before has any small body of ordinary people so moved the world that their enemies could say, with tears of rage in their eyes, that these men 'have turned the world upside down'. (J. B. Phillips, *The Young Church in Action*, Bles, 1955)

Spirit of courage

The disciples were ordinary men with presumably no more than average courage. When Jesus was captured and crucified, the disciples were distraught, their hopes and dreams in tatters. After Pentecost, Luke repeatedly emphasises a distinctive new quality. They don't whisper in secret their loyalty to Jesus, behind locked doors. They proclaim the good news far and wide, 'with boldness' and 'with power'. Peter and John are soon seized by the Jewish authorities. They are told in no uncertain terms to give up evangelism (Acts 4:1–20). The response of the young Church is not to disband or become a secret society, but to pray. In their prayer they ask for a fresh filling of the Spirit. This is not merely to give them new peace of mind, nor is it to protect them from arrest. Their first concern is not their own safety at all, but the unhindered proclamation of the gospel: 'Enable your servants to speak your word with great boldness' (4:29).

Sure enough, when the Spirit comes, they are filled once more and all the believers 'spoke the word of God boldly' (4:31). Again Peter and John are arrested. Again the Sanhedrin command them not to preach about Jesus. And again Peter and John claim that their preaching comes from a higher authority, who cannot be disobeyed in order to please other people. They explain that the chief witness to Jesus is the Holy Spirit. Because he witnesses and lives in them, they must witness too. The Sanhedrin can command them all they like, but they simply cannot give up speaking about Jesus (5:32). The end of Acts 5 confirms that this was no empty bravado. 'Day after day' the apostles preach, in public in the temple courts and in private from house to house (5:42). And day by day, despite all the threats and despite what has happened to Jesus so recently, new converts continue to be added to the Church (6:1).

When the Christians were emboldened, the Jewish authorities were astonished. Other self-styled Messianic leaders had arisen in recent years. Some had been inevitably been unmasked as frauds in their lifetime. Others had kept up appearances until death, but then their followers drifted away (5:36-7). Jesus's disciples had lain low for the first few weeks after his death. The authorities must have hoped that the Galilean problem was already past history, but no sooner were Peter and John released than they were back on the streets. Their courage was no flash in the pan. No threats could silence them.

The astonishment went still deeper, for these men of new courage took on the leading minds of Jerusalem in theological debate. Thanks to the unbeatable combination of Jesus's teaching and the Spirit's inspiration, they had a remarkable grasp of the Old Testament and a new understanding of the promised Messiah. They claimed that Jesus was no less than God's own Son, and that now, raised from the dead, he was pouring out his Spirit on his followers. Experience, understanding of the Scriptures and a new way of living all meshed together. They spoke with remarkable confidence and authority, despite the well-known fact that they were 'unschooled, ordinary men' (4:13), and everyone knew that unlettered fishermen simply don't do that kind of thing!

Still more remarkable, this new theological insight was combined with great clarity in preaching and popular appeal. Holding their own with the Jerusalem academics, the disciples of Jesus also managed to communicate on the right wavelength with the crowds. For courage and persistence, for clear insight and persuasive preaching, the disciples had the Sanhedrin bemused. It was just as they had been promised. The Spirit would come in power, he would give the right words to say (Mark 13:11), and he would glorify Jesus (John 16:14).

Signs and wonders

It wasn't just through new courage and new preaching that the Spirit witnessed to Jesus. At Pentecost, the miraculous gift of tongues drew an enormous crowd, and led to the conversion of three thousand people. A little while later, Peter and John were stopped at the Temple's Beautiful Gate by a beggar crippled from birth (Acts 3). They had no money to offer, but he was healed in Jesus's name. Once more a crowd gathered, Peter preached, and the Church grew to five thousand (4:4).

Where the Spirit is at work, outsiders begin to take notice. They start asking questions, and evangelistic preaching provides the answers. The Spirit causes the event, draws the crowd, inspires the explanation, and in all of this he glorifies Jesus. Signs and wonders were not freakish or fringe activities among the first Christians. When they prayed for the Spirit to give boldness in preaching, they also prayed for miracles – 'Stretch out your hand to heal and perform miraculous signs and wonders through the name of your holy servant Jesus' (4:30). Sure enough, the same Spirit provided them both with boldness and with miracles.

Luke reports that there were many signs and wonders in Jerusalem (Acts 5:12–16). The believers met regularly at Solomon's colonnade, and crowds gathered before them, bringing their sick to be healed. These miracles were not some kind of showmanship to draw a crowd. They were genuine, supernatural and practical expressions of the love of God. Just as Jesus had healed out of pure love, there is no suggestion that the disciples only prayed for healing for those already converted. The great desire of the first Christians was to see as many as possible receive forgiveness and enter the new age of the Spirit through saving faith in Christ. The signs and wonders were dramatic demonstrations of God's love for men and women.

When the Church ignores signs and wonders, it's as if we have erased all the verses about healing and deliverance from the New Testament. We begin to act as if they simply don't exist. Stephen is remembered by many as the first Christian martyr and one of the first deacons (Acts 6). He was a great preacher, and when the authorities seized him, he preached a heroic martyr's sermon. All of this is quite well known. But Stephen's ministry was no mere administrative post on the Jerusalem church's food committee. Luke also emphasises that Stephen was 'full of faith and of the Holy Spirit' (6:5), and 'full of God's grace and power' he 'did great wonders and miraculous signs among the people' (6:8). It wasn't a ministry reserved for the apostles; a more junior leader was involved in miracles as well. Signs and wonders were the common fare of the first Christians. As J. B. Phillips observed, 'They did not hold conferences on psycho-somatic medicine; they simply healed the sick' (*The Young Church in Action*).

Full of the Spirit in his preaching and full of the Spirit in his signs and wonders, Stephen is full of the Spirit again at the moment of martyrdom (Acts 7:55). It is then that he receives his wonderful vision of Jesus 'standing at the right hand of God'. Once again the Spirit is true to himself and his task. Through the vision, the glorification of Jesus is once again confirmed and Stephen is inspired, in the face of death, to bear the courageous witness of a Christian martyr. Stephen's warning is a stark reminder to those who prefer their religion respectable and a Spirit-free zone: to reject the message is to resist the Spirit, and to resist the Spirit is to reject the living God (7:51).

As the Church spread, signs and wonders spread with it. Paul refers in his letters to 'signs following' and 'demonstrations of the Spirit's power' as the normative pattern of his ministry (Rom. 15:19; 2 Cor. 12:12; 1 Thess. 1:5). Luke records that when Paul and Barnabas preached at Iconium, they made a good initial impression on both Jews and Gentiles, but those Jews who rejected the message stirred up opposition. As at Jerusalem, instead of going underground to save their own skins, Paul and Barnabas were inspired by the Spirit, 'speaking boldly for the Lord'. Luke has shown previously that signs and wonders can gather a crowd. Now he describes how they can also follow preaching, authenticating in dramatic experience the presence of God and the gospel of grace: 'The Lord . . . confirmed the message of his grace by enabling them to do miraculous signs and wonders' (Acts 14:3).

Signs and wonders didn't just declare the love of God and confirm the message of Christ. They also helped prevent the Church from becoming racist or sectarian. In Acts 15 the Church reached a crisis. As numbers grew, and more Gentiles were converted, the original Jewish Christians had to decide whether the Gentiles were their equals in Christ, or still needed to be circumcised and come under the law of Israel. Two key contributions to the debate come from Peter and Paul. They do not begin with debates about theological principles or human initiatives and policies. Instead, they describe the surprising acts of the Spirit. Peter cites the gift of the Spirit to Cornelius, which convinced him that God 'made no distinction between us and them' (15:9). When Paul and Barnabas speak, they don't concentrate on examples of individual Gentile conversions. Instead they confirm that the gospel of Christ is for all by telling of their missionary experiences. They don't have slides to project or samples of Gentile handicraft, but they can tell of something both vivid and memorable. God has been at work, and his method, just like at Jerusalem, has been to use signs and wonders: 'The whole assembly became silent as they listened to Barnabas and Paul telling about the miraculous signs and wonders God had done among the Gentiles through them' (15:12).

This power is both exciting and awesome. Simon the sorcerer knew his own trickery was no match for it (Acts 8:9–24). Such power was enviable, and could be the means to much money and fame. He did as any charlatan would, and tried to buy the Spirit from Peter. He made a double mistake. No man controls the Spirit of God, not even the foundational apostles. What is more, the Spirit is only given by God to those who repent and are baptised into Christ. The Spirit is never fuel for profit in a commercial enterprise, and he can never be bought and sold (8:20–23).

Signs and wonders aren't important in Acts solely in the context of evangelism, but that seems to be their primary setting. Signs and wonders aren't a necessary part of every evangelistic activity, but they are remarkably frequent in the early Church. Through the presence and power of the Spirit, signs and wonders glorify Jesus as Lord. It would be dangerously easy to overstate the role of signs and wonders in the New Testament, for they did not occur at every single evangelistic event and there was clearly an equally important place for reasoned argument in defence of the gospel. Nor did they automatically guarantee mass conversions. But for most churches this romanticised exaggeration of the place of signs and wonders is not the most pressing problem. Instead, Western Christians have often read the Bible as if signs and wonders never happened at all.

Faced with frequent signs and wonders in the early Church we must ask some uncomfortable questions. Is our reading of the New Testament selective? Do we pick and choose the activities of the Spirit that we are comfortable with, approving these and ignoring the rest? If we do, we risk rejecting not just those activities but the Spirit himself, and, as Stephen warned, those who resist the Spirit are doing no less than resisting God.

The Jerusalem church left the Jewish authorities with a big problem. Everyone in Jerusalem knew about the healing of the cripple at the Beautiful Gate (Acts 4:16), and crowds from beyond Jerusalem soon began to bring their sick for healing and deliverance (5:16). Signs and wonders were hot news that backed up the proclamation of the risen Christ. Many didn't understand the new age of the Spirit, but the opponents of the Christians couldn't deny they had remarkable power. They didn't have to ask, 'What difference does it make if you become a Christian?' They could see its results with their own eyes.

Paul's mission in the Spirit

In the second half of Acts, Luke concentrates on Paul's ministry, but this doesn't diminish his emphasis on the Holy Spirit. Struck blind by the vision of Jesus on the Damascus Road, Saul was commanded to wait in the city for instructions, which he did for three days, while praying and fasting (Acts 9:6, 9). Poor Ananias. He knew all about Saul, one of the most notorious persecutors of the Christians. Now he was commanded by the Lord in a vision to go and pray for him (9:10–12). Ananias protested at first, but eventually relented. When he prayed for his new brother in Christ, Paul's sight was restored, he was filled with the Spirit and he received through Ananias the prophetic word that he would evangelise the Gentiles (9:15, 17–19). Paul had thought he was serving the God of Israel by persecuting Christians. When the Spirit came upon him, he could at last see clearly that to serve God meant to proclaim Jesus as Lord and Saviour, to the ends of the earth.

Luke is also at pains to stress the crucial role of the Spirit in the development of Paul's ministry. When the leadership team at Antioch were worshipping and fasting, they decided to set aside two of their key leaders for out-of-town missions. This wasn't a pre-planned decision of the team, but came instead as a result of the Spirit speaking through a prophetic word (13:2). The Holy Spirit stayed involved in Paul's missionary journeys: it was the Spirit who kept him from preaching in Asia (16:6), the Spirit who compelled him to go to Jerusalem (20:22); the Spirit who warned him 'in every city' of the 'prison and hardships' to be faced at Jerusalem (20:23); and the Spirit who alerted him through the prophet Agabus that the Jews would bind Paul and hand him over to the Romans for trial (21:11–13). Paul never sought an easy way out, for he realised from the time of his conversion that the Spirit was not given to preserve his own skin – 'I will show him how much he must suffer for my name' (9:16). The presence of the Holy Spirit invites, equips and inspires Paul to be devoted to his particular calling in the mission of the Church – 'testifying to the gospel of God's grace' (20:24).

The presence of the Spirit is an acid test of true conversion. Modern Christians might typically ask, 'Have you become a Christian?' or 'Have you been born again?' When Paul met some followers of John the Baptist from Ephesus, he had a different question: 'Did you receive the Holy Spirit when you believed?' (19:2). It's not that Paul thought all Christians should go through carbon copies of his own experience, but he was quite clear that the presence of the Spirit is the hallmark of every true Christian.

The Ephesians confessed that they didn't even know there was a Holy Spirit. Their understanding was as deficient as their faith. Like those who strenuously make new year resolutions they had repented of the past, but they had no confidence of forgiveness, no new encounter with God, and no new inner resources for future change. Repentance on its own is never enough, and is far less than the full gospel of Jesus Christ. As a result, Paul had to teach them not only about the Holy Spirit but first about the need to believe in Christ. He took them right back to basics, and when they responded with living faith, he baptised them. This is very significant, because it is the only time in Acts when people seem at first sight to have been 'rebaptised'. Paul was quite clear that John's baptism is not enough, because it is not the same as full Christian baptism. All Christians need to be baptised not just for repentance but as a result and expression of saving faith in Christ. Far more important than water baptism, all Christians need to be fully immersed in the Holy Spirit, and so Paul then placed his hands upon them in prayer, and they were duly filled.

Almost all Christian churches accept the importance of water baptism, even though many fail to follow the New Testament pattern of baptising believers. But the greater need of being filled with the Spirit has often been ignored or underplayed. Just imagine the fuss in some churches or denominational gatherings if Paul asked the same blunt question of today's badly birthed believers: 'Did you receive the Spirit when you believed?' Receiving the Holy Spirit is essential for every believer.

Christians are sometimes known as *the people who don't* . . . don't drink . . . don't smoke . . . don't smile . . . don't know how to have fun. In Acts, the Christians are more alive than ever before. Paul simply couldn't see the Christian difference in these Ephesians, and so he asked them about the Spirit. We need to ask whether our non-Christian friends can see any positive difference in us. The Ephesians replied that they didn't know the Spirit existed. Once I would have offered a different reply: 'Well, Paul, I know there is a Holy Spirit, but our church prefers not to talk about that.' All too often Christians have behaved as if the Spirit is not a suitable subject for polite conversation. Nothing in the New Testament can possibly justify such appalling avoidance of the Spirit of God.

Every Christian witness

Although Luke concentrates mainly on the exploits of Peter and Paul in the power of the Spirit, he never suggests that God only works through high-profile leaders. Not all are called to be like Peter, Paul, or even Billy Graham. But the Spirit enables all to be faithful witnesses to Christ, in both life and words. Changed lives will be noticed, and people will ask for explanations. In Acts chapter 8, the ordinary Christians prove just as courageous for Jesus when, after Stephen's martyrdom, the Jerusalem church is scattered under fierce persecution. Rather than going underground to protect themselves, they 'preached the word wherever they went' (8:4).

Luke records open-air meetings and organised debates. There is witness in public and witness in homes. Chance meetings on journeys become opportunities for evangelism. Even arrest can lead to more people hearing the gospel. The new age of the Spirit is marked by the desire to proclaim the gospel and by a steady stream of new church plants as churches established by the apostles assume a regional church-planting responsibility. There is no single technique or method of witnessing used by every Christian in every situation, but all are called, in many different ways, to testify to the grace of Christ. We cannot be truly open to the Spirit without being ready and willing to be active witnesses for Jesus. The Spirit never distracts Christians from mission to a needy world, in fact he promotes it. The age of the Spirit is the age of evangelism.

11

What God has joined together

Radio phone-ins can be relied on for one thing: if two experts are in the studio, each caller will receive two quite different answers. The hardy perennials of *Gardeners' Question Time* take it further. One expert praises chemical additives. A second advises double digging, or something equally energetic. Then comes a third reply, full of Latin names for plants, recommending countless varieties in preference to the one the questioner is struggling to grow. Up-to-date gardeners are all about trace elements and systemic insecticide. Traditionalists seem dedicated to muscular activity, unable even to enjoy their blooms without breaking into a sweat. But the scientist still needs his spade, just as no double-digger can be complete without his fertiliser.

When it comes to the Spirit, Christians often slip into opposite camps. What God has joined together, we divide. The Spirit is set in needless conflict with the Word or the mind, with tradition or with matter. This risks dividing us from each other, from inner wholeness, and ultimately even from the Spirit himself. These problems aren't new. They were already arising and being dealt with in the days of the New Testament.

Spirit and Word

Paul is quite clear. The Spirit breathed Scripture into life. That doesn't mean he dictated it, but every sentence of the Bible has double authorship; it is the book of God and of human writers.

God inspired the Scriptures with a unique authority, so that they teach us reliably about himself, rebuke our self-centredness, and train us in living for Jesus (2 Tim. 3:16). The Spirit created the Bible, and he knew what he was doing. For the first Christians, the Spirit didn't replace the Old Testament. He made it more clear, more relevant, more practical and more alive than it had ever been before. When Paul got up from the Damascus Road he didn't give away his scrolls of the Old Testament. He pored over them more than ever, as they helped him understand Christ and as Christ's coming helped him understand the Scriptures. His letters are full of quotations from the Old Testament, even as the gospel writers take great pleasure in quoting the Old Testament to demonstrate just how many prophecies have been fulfilled in Christ.

Jesus spelt out the Spirit's crucial role in the composition of the gospels. The gospels would depend on the living Spirit, not on mere human memory. The Spirit would not dictate the gospels word for word, but Jesus promised that the Spirit would enliven the memories of the eyewitnesses, helping them to remember all that Jesus taught. More than that, the Spirit of Truth was also coming to illumine those memories, clarifying their significance and applying them to the present needs of the Church (John 14:26). Jesus therefore explains that the Spirit is the reason for the authority and up-to-dateness of the Bible. He has inspired writings that are uniquely and universally true. What is more, as we saw in chapter 3, the Spirit of truth would continue to teach all things. He wouldn't shut up shop after Pentecost, but would explain why Jesus had to die. In every generation, the Lord has yet more light to shed upon and through his Word.

Jesus quoted the Old Testament in order to explain what it means to live a Spirit-filled life. At the beginning of his public ministry he claimed for himself Isaiah's prophetic description of the consequences of the Spirit of the Lord coming upon an individual. Different denominations and streams tend to have their own instinctive emphases when describing the characteristics of Spirit-filled leadership. Jesus invites us to move beyond the limits of our particular religious sub-culture and use the yardstick of Scripture as the reliable test of any aspirations to a Spirit-filled ministry.

> The Spirit of the Lord is on me,
>> because he has anointed me
>> to preach good news to the poor.
> He has sent me to proclaim freedom for the prisoners
>> and recovery of sight for the blind,
>> to release the oppressed,
>> to proclaim the year of the Lord's favour.
> (Luke 4:18–19 quoting Isa. 61:1–2)

The Spirit never speaks in a voice contrary to Scripture, but he does have the power to make the unchanging and universal truths of the Bible directly and personally relevant. We need the Spirit's living presence to make Scripture more than a dead letter on the page, and as he does so, the centre of attention will always be Jesus. We must draw a fundamental distinction between the Spirit illumining the Scriptures and the disastrous error of illuminism. The Spirit delights in wielding his Sword of Truth, which is the Word he has inspired, so that Bible verses and doctrines cut through our dull-wittedness to speak to every circumstance of life. Whether in conversion, daily living or even in momentous events like the Reformation, when the truths of Scripture swept across Europe with a new-found clarity and authority, the revelation that the Holy Spirit illumines is the truth found in Scripture.

In illuminism, however, a person declares that they have received a revelation from the Holy Spirit that either makes the Bible obsolete or, and this is still more beguiling to some gullible followers, interprets the Scriptures in a totally new and unorthodox way. Such 'revelations' not only ignore or overturn the natural meaning of Scripture, they also require a by-pass of the human mind, since any attempt at a reasoned exploration of the new teaching is customarily repudiated as ungodliness. Illuminism is a hot-house of subjective religious impressions where anything may be taught, the more exotic and bizarre the better. Such fevered speculative theology is far removed from the work of the Holy Spirit who faithfully and reliably illumines the Scriptures. The Lord always has new light to shed upon his Word, but the Holy Spirit cannot possibly be behind any attempt to marginalise or ignore the Scriptures he has inspired.

When the New Testament was complete, the Spirit didn't withdraw. In every generation, he lights up the Bible afresh. For every

Christian, he gives inner witness that in the Bible, God has spoken. The old saying remains true: 'If you have the Word without the Spirit, you dry up. If you have the Spirit without the Word, you blow up. But if you have both together, you grow up!' The same Spirit now makes Scripture unmistakably alive. He won't contradict what he has already inspired. If someone declares that the Spirit has revealed to them something that contradicts or demeans the Bible, their inspiration has certainly not come from the Spirit of God.

This takes us to the broader issue of the Scriptures and spiritual experiences. On the one hand, the Bible always points beyond itself to experiences of the Spirit: it is never enough, biblically, to know about God in theory. The sufficiency of the Scriptures means that all that needs to be revealed for our salvation is to be found in the Bible. It certainly does not mean that the Scriptures are sufficient as an end in themselves, rendering all experiences of God's presence and love invalid or superfluous. The words of the Bible constantly point beyond themselves to personal encounter with the living God. However, when we enjoy experiences of the Spirit, as he comes to us in love or peace, power or joy, we then need to understand that our experiences of the Spirit must be interpreted by the Scriptures. In this way our experiences are properly tested, so that we can sort out the genuine from mere human excitement or excess. Our experiences of the Spirit will help us understand the Scriptures better. But we must strenuously avoid the danger of hyper-subjectivism that arises if Scripture is bent over backwards to conform to the pattern of our dreams, visions and intuitions. That way lies sub-Christian mysticism rather than authentic evangelicalism. No matter how strenuously someone declares that the Holy Spirit is providing them with their revelation, if the content is not biblical the inspiration cannot come from the Spirit of God. Experience must be interpreted in the light of Christ and not Christ in the light of experience.

Many people have a tendency to jump to hasty conclusions. In his *Book of Martyrs* John Foxe told how Thomas Cranmer used a very different method to rediscover the truths of the gospel: 'before he would addict his mind to any opinion, he spent three whole years reading over the books of Holy Scripture.' The psalmist speaks in a similar vein of storing up God's word in our hearts in order to protect ourselves from sin (Ps. 119:11). There is no substitute for investing in the Word of God. The Spirit does not provide a short cut to avoid the effort. Rather, he gives us the determination to keep on digging deeper in the Bible. One of the most important decisions I made as a student was to attempt to read the whole Bible each summer vacation: the Spirit stirs within us a hunger to know God's Word better.

Preachers have a high privilege and grave responsibility when it comes to the Bible. The good preacher will root every message in the Scriptures, building up in a congregation over the years a growing understanding of the whole counsel of God. The kind of preaching that ignores the Bible, concentrating exclusively on inspiring stories and amusing anecdotes is a pale imitation of the real thing. The Holy Spirit stirs up the preacher not to tickle his hearers' ears with religious entertainment but to help them be rooted firmly in the Word of God. Accept no substitutes: true preaching is thoroughly biblical and Spirit-empowered. We need nothing less in preaching than Word and Spirit together. In this way we will know the true nourishment and lasting inspiration of truth on fire.

Many centuries ago, a philosopher called Origen summed up to a young Christian how the Spirit and the Bible go together: 'Do you then, my son, diligently apply yourself to the reading of the sacred Scriptures. Apply yourself, I say. For we who read the things of God need much application, lest we should say or think anything too rashly about them . . . And applying yourself thus to the divine study, seek aright . . . for prayer is of all things indispensable to the knowledge of the things of God.'

The Spirit inspired and illumines the Word, and the Word points beyond itself to the Spirit. The apostle Paul also revealed that the Spirit is the devoted guardian of the Scriptures he has inspired. When we accept the apostolic task of guarding and defending the gospel in our generation, we can do so with the Spirit's constant help (2 Tim. 1:14). Spirit or Word? God has given both. And we need both.

Spirit and mind

Some Christians seem to suggest that the Holy Spirit makes the human brain redundant. Others almost seem to require a university entrance exam for conversion. The book of Proverbs walks a tightrope between underrating and overrating the human mind.

Through searching and discipline a man can find wisdom (Prov. 3:11–13). But he must not lean on his own understanding (3:5). True wisdom begins with the fear of the Lord, in whose presence intellectual pride is shown to be nonsense. Self-confidence is replaced by trust in the Lord, who gives his wisdom to the faithful.

It isn't that the mind is worthless. But it needs to be harnessed in humble service of God. When it claims to be self-sufficient and its own master, trouble is sure to follow. John Newman faced this temptation while studying at Oxford. Later he wrote, 'I was beginning to prefer intellectual excellence to moral; I was drifting . . .' Knowledge about God risked becoming more important than love for God. That would be disastrous, and Newman swiftly repented the fault. Learning was not evicted, but was made afresh the junior partner to Christian devotion.

When men and women rely on their minds alone, they create a god in their own image. Any theology that is rooted in human pride cannot grow beyond dead theory. Paul warned the Ephesians, 'No longer live as the Gentiles do, in the futility of their thinking' (Eph. 4:17). Liberal theology that rules out the possibilities of supernatural intervention demonstrates this intellectual paralysis. If you presuppose that God does not intervene in human history, it is quite impossible to make good sense of all the evidence for the historical resurrection of Christ. But it is not only liberalism that can suffer from futile thinking: we can also identify a mutant form of evangelicalism that is severely attenuated by the constraints of rationalism.

We need to make a sharp distinction between a reasonable faith and a rationalistic faith. Peter clearly believed that Christians could give good reasons for their convictions, for he gave this clear instruction: 'Always be prepared to give an answer to everyone who asks you to give the reason for the hope that you have' (1 Pet. 3:15). A reasonable faith is built on a set of convictions that can be presented, defended and examined reasonably. Every Christian should be capable of explaining the evidence for the resurrection and the reasons for our conviction that Jesus really was and is the Son of God and the Saviour of the world. A rationalistic faith, however, is a set of religious convictions circumscribed or contained within the limits of the rational mind. A rationalistic faith is therefore at best uncomfortable and at worst suspicious, dismissive or censorious faced with any claims to a personal encounter with God's love or healing power. The Holy Spirit is the great disruptor; throughout church history his presence has violated the good order of respectable religion. He cannot possibly be contained within the narrow and deadening confines of rationalistic religion. Liberalism is a form of rationalistic religion and a child of the enlightenment, but so is that frigid perversion of warm-blooded evangelicalism that rules out any present-day outpourings of the Holy Spirit: it is a dead orthodoxy, holding to the form of sound religion while denying its power (2 Tim. 3:5).

The same Paul who warned against idle speculation also wrote the letter to the Romans. This contains the most detailed New Testament exploration of the meaning of the gospel. In that context he urges, 'be transformed by the renewing of your mind' (Rom.12:2). To be sure, Paul refers to our basic attitudes and instincts, but also to our understanding. God in Christ can renew the whole mind, because in Christ he has redeemed the whole person. Luther was converted through reading Romans, and he never grew tired of its stimulus to the Christian mind: 'It can never be read or pondered too much, and the more it is dealt with the more precious it becomes, and the better it tastes.'

In 1 Corinthians, Paul explains that no one can fully know the thoughts of another. In the same way, the human mind on its own cannot understand the mind of God. Therefore, to the unbeliever, the gospel seems foolish. However, the Spirit of God 'searches all things, even the deep things of God' (1 Cor. 2:10). He can reveal spiritual truths beyond the grasp of the unaided human mind. And he is given to Christians to bring those truths home: so that 'we may understand what God has freely given us' (2:12). Paul stresses the limits of the human mind on its own. But he also stresses the renewal and transformation of the mind through the Spirit. Because God's Spirit is now within us, Paul can say that God is each Christian's 'instructor on the inside'. This means that together, 'we have the mind of Christ' (2:16). The Spirit is by no means just interested in academic theology, but we can never claim his support for being anti-intellectual. As John Stott appealed: 'Dear friend, never denigrate truth! Never disdain theology! Never despise your mind! If you do, you grieve the Holy Spirit of Truth' (*The Bible: Book for Today*, IVP, 1982).

Some early Christians found Paul's letters rather complicated, and 2 Peter is sympathetic to their difficulties: 'His letters contain some things that are hard to understand, which ignorant and unstable people distort, as they do the other Scriptures, to their own destruction' (2 Pet. 3:16). Because Paul is sometimes difficult, it doesn't mean he has stopped depending on the Spirit. But at the same time, those who find it a struggle to follow his arguments are by no means spiritually second rate. I remember one Christian man who had never been successful at school exams. His minister was one of those brilliant people who could study for extra degrees as a hobby. Sadly, the chap without qualifications came to equate spirituality with brain power, and thought he was somehow closer to God by struggling out of his depth in highbrow theology. Jesus didn't say, 'Go to university, suitable or not.' He said, 'Follow me.' If God has given you a first-class brain, don't be reluctant to use it, but always make sure you depend on his Spirit. And if your brain power is no more than average, thank God for it, and continue to exercise it for him, relying on the same Spirit. Whatever our level of academic achievement, God's purpose is full employment for every Christian mind.

John Donne wrote that truth stands, 'on a huge hill, cragged and steep'. The indispensable guide to truth's mountain is the Holy Spirit, but a great deal of mental exertion will still be required to scale the heights. Timothy Dwight, in his 1808 inaugural address at Andover Seminary in the United States, spelt out the need for determined and sustained effort in the development of a Christian mind, rebutting the prejudice of those believers who were instinctively anti-intellectual: 'While they demand a seven-year apprenticeship, for the purpose of learning to make a shoe, or an axe, they suppose the system of Providence, together with the numerous, and frequently abstruse, doctrines and precepts, contained in the Scriptures, may all be comprehended without learning, labour, or time.'

A fine expression of this integration of rigorous thinking and spiritual devotion is the prayer used by John Calvin before his lectures at Geneva. His mind was brilliant, but he refused to stray from dependence on God's inspiration and help: 'May the Lord grant that we study the heavenly mysteries of his wisdom, making true progress in religion to his glory and our upbuilding. Amen.'

When Paul prayed for the Philippians, he prayed not only that 'love may abound more and more', but also that this love might abound 'in knowledge and depth of insight' (Phil. 1:9). Paul recognised that the same Holy Spirit is concerned with understanding as well as love, and so his prayer encompasses both head and heart. In the same way, he prays for the Ephesians' minds – that they may comprehend the enormity of God's love in Christ – but also for their hearts – to encounter this love that surpasses knowledge (Eph. 3:16–19). The longest journey truth has to make in many Christians is the journey from head to heart. But Paul doesn't pray for a head by-pass or a heart by-pass. He is eagerly concerned that our minds may be exercised to the full in exploring the glorious extravagance of divine grace, but he also prays that our encounters with this holy love will go way beyond the capacity of our minds, as God's overwhelming love is repeatedly poured into our hearts. Spirit and mind? The one is given to enrich the other. We need to use our minds to the full *and* live in the Spirit to the full.

Spirit and tradition

For many Christians, the authority of the Bible is clear for every generation. But what about tradition? In a world that is constantly changing, what is the value of yesterday? David Watson used to tell the story of visiting a church where the churchwarden announced that he had held office for twenty-five years. 'You must have seen many changes in your time,' David observed. 'Yes,' came the reply. 'And I've resisted every single one of them!' Those who live in the past are dead to the future. When we hold fast to the promise that God is doing a new thing (Isa. 43:18–19), we naturally steer clear of churches stuck in the past. But if we ignore the past, we neglect its wisdom and are condemned to repeat its mistakes.

A local church had some rather unattractive late Victorian lettering on the front wall. You noticed it was old-fashioned more than what it actually said. But when it finally came to redecorating they would retouch it 'same as it has always been'. Bad tradition eventually turns a church into a museum. But in 1 Corinthians 11, Paul reveals a vital tradition. What the Lord had passed on to Paul, he has passed on to each local church, and now repeats to the Corinthians. This tradition is the words of the institution of the Lord's Supper, and ever since the words handed on to the Corinthians have been preserved and handed on to every church in every nation and century. In the same way, whatever translation we use, when we pray the Lord's Prayer we echo the prayer that Jesus gave, which has been benefiting his disciples in a living tradition across the generations.

The Spirit has always been present in Christ's Church. Just as he teaches us the meaning of Scripture, he has given rich insight to previous generations. The early Christians spoke of the Rule of Faith, in which the doctrine and practical instruction of the Bible was summed up. Our own Bible studies are never infallible, and nor is tradition. But tested against the Bible, we should expect the wisdom of past Christians to be 'helpful as a guide, much more right than wrong' (J. I. Packer, essay in *Scripture and Truth*, D. Carson and J. Woodbridge (Eds.), IVP, 1983).

There are two arrogant attitudes towards the past. First what C. S. Lewis called 'chronological snobbery'. That means assuming that the latest is always the best, which is, of course, a common attitude in our fast-moving and proud modern culture. The book of Proverbs tells us to respect the wisdom of past generations, and the Holy Spirit invites us to hear echoes of his voice through their ways of living and patterns of thought. In its most extreme form, this prejudice gives rise to hyper-radicalism, in which great pleasure is taken in being so different from every other church that no one beyond an exclusive élite can make any sense of a wacky style of worship. To these ultimate exponents of chronological snobbery, trendiness is next to godliness.

The second arrogant attitude arose as an unintentional side-effect of the Reformation. Because tradition had claimed for itself supreme authority, Luther had to confront it with Scripture. He reclaimed final authority for the gospel of grace. Ever since, some Protestants, especially free-church evangelicals, have tended to swing to the opposite extreme of assuming that tradition must always, or nearly always, be automatically wrong. Tradition is guilty unless proved innocent. This raises a problem. If the Church has consistently misheard the Spirit in the past, how can we have any real confidence that we are hearing him accurately today?

In correcting tradition, Luther never dismissed the value of truly biblical insights from the past. The Christian who refuses to learn from the words and writings of others depends on his own pride more than on the Spirit. Jim Packer has warned of churches 'whose interpretative style, though disciplined and conscientious, is narrow, shallow, naive, lacking in roots, and wooden to a fault, for want of encounter with the theological and expository wisdom of nineteen Christian centuries' (essay in *Scripture and Truth*).

John Wesley refused to be tied down to conventional methods of preaching and evangelism. He was therefore no prisoner of the past, yet he devoted much time, energy and money to republishing Christian classics. As an addition to Bible reading he encouraged regular study of the best Christian books of every age. They are a supplementary diet of spiritual stimulus and wisdom, provided for us in the goodness of God. Drawing on the inspiration of Wesley's publishing initiative, during my time in charge of Hodder Christian books I launched the Hodder Christian Classics series as a modern-day initiative to make the best devotional books of every generation readily and inexpensively available for Christians today.

It's the same with hymns. Some seem to think that you can only worship God through hymns written before the war – sometimes before the Boer War! Others think something is only 'of the Spirit' if it was written since 1995. Neither age nor youthfulness is any guarantee of true spirituality! Some old hymns are dead weight in the hymnbooks, and some modern songs are undeniably dreadful. But the one Spirit has given fresh songs in every age. Some are useful only for a few years, but others stay full of spiritual vitality for centuries. We need to rejoice in all that the Spirit has given in the past, and in all that he is giving today. Only pride can presume to ascribe the outer limits of true worship to 'the way we do it round here', and true wisdom to our own culture and generation.

Once we have recognised that the Spirit of God has been at work in every generation of Christians, we also need to face the crisis of irrelevance facing the Western church at the end of the twentieth century. As I argued in *21st Century Church* (Hodder and Stoughton, 1994), the modern world will not be reached effectively by traditional forms of the Church. The message doesn't change, but the Church is always needing to reinvent itself as a culturally engaged embodiment of the gospel. The Spirit is always our contemporary, and so, while we have much to learn from the past, we cannot serve Christ effectively in our own day by attempting to live in the past.

Our church in Wimbledon is a thoroughly contemporary church, and I am delighted to be released from the tyranny of irrelevant church traditions. However, while I am fully committed to the need for radical and creative cultural engagement, I am also thoroughly convinced that the Spirit who leads us today has guided the Church into the truth of Christ in every generation. As a result, while my office is in an attractive and purpose-built modern building, many of the most important books in my library are the great Christian classics of previous centuries, in devotion and doctrine, biography and Bible commentaries.

In respecting the past, we respect our parents, and our forebears. That may not be very fashionable in a culture addicted to modernity, but it is an inescapable and natural implication of the fifth commandment. The Spirit invites us to recognise that he has been guiding Christians in every generation. If we test the past by Scripture, we honour the Spirit. If we reject the past out of hand, we reject what the Spirit has done among past generations of Christians. When we marginalise the past, we marginalise the past work of the Spirit of Truth.

Spirit and matter

Israel's neighbours made up many myths about creation in which a god of order waged war with a goddess of chaos. But Genesis 1 affirms that Yahweh is the only God. By him alone all things were made, and all that he made is good. That means that God is interested in the natural world and the whole of life, not just the parts we sometimes think are 'spiritual' or 'religious'.

The Corinthian Christians were into exotic spiritual experiences. If it was sensational, they wanted it, and they really thought they had arrived. Paul had to remind them that the marks of the apostles were not success or spiritual highs so much as devotion to God and persecution. Spiritual living means, above all else, putting into practice the Sermon on the Mount – 'We are fools for Christ . . . we are in rags, we are brutally treated, we are homeless . . . when we are cursed, we bless; when we are persecuted, we endure it; when we are slandered, we answer kindly' (1 Cor. 4:10–13). The Corinthian problems went still deeper. They were so concerned about things 'spiritual', that they thought sin didn't really matter any more. They got involved in all kinds of degrading and foolish behaviour. What was more, just like their Greek neighbours, they looked forward to death as the moment when the soul escaped from the prison of the body. Paul had to remind them that while the old and sinful nature must be crucified, God had saved their bodies as well as their souls. The new temple of the Holy Spirit is not other-worldly; it is the physical body of every Christian (6:19). What is more, just as Jesus left the tomb in a bodily resurrection, beyond death all who are in Christ will receive a resurrection body (15:42-4). God didn't simply provide us with earthly bodies, he will even give us replacement ones for heaven.

The Colossians had a similar problem. They too tried to oppose the Spirit to matter, and became addicted to other-worldliness. Some took delight in describing their visionary experiences at great length. Others got involved in some kind of mystical, fanciful and super-spiritual angel worship (Col. 2:18). Paul called this super-spirituality a set of 'idle notions'. Worse still, they combined their 'hollow and deceptive philosophy' (2:8) with legalism. To free their souls for visions, they tried to tie down their bodies with countless laws: 'Do not handle! Do not taste! Do not touch!' (2:21). Where the Corinthians indulged in lawlessness, the Colossians came into terrible legalistic bondage. Paul would have none of it. He knew that 'harsh treatment of the body' lacks 'any value in restraining sensual indulgence' (Col. 2:23). A heart-change was needed, and that could only be provided by Christ through his Spirit. The Colossians needed to pray for practical renewal on the inside, and turn from their obsession with visions and angels.

To drive home his point, Paul invited them to reconsider the incarnation. The Colossians found bodies so distasteful that they began to think of Christ as a sort of spiritual apparition, without any real body at all. For Paul, this was unthinkable, and so he spelt out the fully human and historical reality of Jesus who was also God: 'In Christ all the fullness of the Deity lives in bodily form' (2:9). The Colossians had thought that spirit and body were like oil and water. Paul insisted not only that God saves us in our human entirety, body, mind and soul, but also that the Son of God took upon himself a fully human form and then took his humanity with him in his ascension to heaven.

The root cause of the prejudices that Paul needed to correct was the pervasive influence across the Roman empire of Platonism. In Platonic thought, the world of the spirit is the world of unchanging ideas, while the material world is in a constant state of change. Life is therefore compartmentalised, with much greater value being placed on the higher, spiritual dimension, while the material realm is indisputably inferior. For many centuries Christians were influenced more than they realised by this cultural and philosophical dualism. As a result they were inclined to separate life into two parts, the secular and the sacred, the bodily and the spiritual. Out of such dualistic thinking, marriage tended to be devalued and sex came to be seen as somehow dirty, while the spiritual people – priests, monks and nuns – lived the higher spiritual life. Celibacy was considered to be intrinsically more spiritual than a sexually active marriage. Such attitudes have no biblical justification whatsoever. In stark contrast to Platonism, C. S. Lewis summed up the high value that biblical thinking gives to the physical world and the physical aspects of human existence: 'God likes matter, he invented it.'

The influence of Platonism in the early Christian centuries may seem rather remote, but its influence was surprisingly long-lasting and its repudiation has crucial implications. It means that God is involved in our everyday world, and not just the religious bits. It means that he is interested in washing up and gardening, as well as prayer and Bible study. It means that my work isn't less important to God if I am in business, rather than what is often mistakenly called 'full-time Christian work', for all suitable work can be full-time Christian work for the committed disciple of Christ. Our highest calling is to live for Christ wherever he wants us to serve: not every Christian receives the particular calling to become a minister or a missionary. Christian discipleship, therefore, means that we have to work out how best to serve Christ in our particular workplace and with our time and money. Holistic discipleship even has implications for such practicalities as a healthy diet and sufficient exercise.

The God who gave us our bodies has made us capable of sporting prowess, and so sportsmen and women can find legitimate and encouraging inspiration for prayer in the source of Samson's astonishing strength: 'The Spirit of the Lord came upon him in power' (Judg. 14:19). Jonathan Edwards, world record holder in the triple jump, has made clear his Christian faith and his sense of divine favour upon his sporting achievements. Eric Liddell, winner of an Olympic gold before dying in a Japanese concentration camp, expressed well this integration of life in the Spirit and sporting excellence: 'I was made to serve God and to run fast. And when I run I can feel God's pleasure.'

God is also interested in natural beauty, for the cosmos is a masterwork of his creativity. This does mean, incidentally, that a poster or painting of exquisitely beautiful scenery is thoroughly Christian without the addition of an appropriate text. God in his wisdom created the trees without Bible verses engraved automatically in their bark: they don't need the addition of words before they can declare his glory. Francis Bacon observed that God has provided two books: the Bible, 'the book of his words', and nature, 'the book of his works'. The scientist explores the mysteries of God's handiwork, discovering the order and beauty with which God has framed creation. The environmentalist discovers and seeks to defend the inter-connectedness of living things: we should be concerned to protect other creatures not simply because they may be useful to us, but because they are in themselves objects of wonder, the handiwork of our Creator. God gave Adam a clear instruction not to exploit or despoil creation, but to be its custodian on behalf of the Creator. The BSE scandal has its origins in a wretched and shameful violation of the natural order: in order to maximise profits, we turned cows into carnivores, forcing them to eat their own kind. We must tirelessly insist that this world belongs to God, and not to accountants. All Christians are called to be Green Christians.

The integrated, life-encompassing vision of the Bible also affirms that God is by no means opposed to art and the imagination. Art needs no justification: painting and sculpture, music and writing, all have intrinsic value and are legitimate Christian pursuits not solely in the context of evangelism or Sunday services. Human creativity comes from the creator God, in whose image we are made. More than that, Christians have within them the very Spirit who brooded over the waters and brought creation into being. Becoming a Christian should therefore never stunt our creativity or make us indifferent to art. God can release our imaginations, and unlock a creativity we never knew before. The same Holy Spirit can open our eyes both to nature and to art.

Spirit and matter? They were brought into decisive harmony in the incarnation. God invented matter and he redeemed it. Every time we celebrate the Lord's Supper we see them working together, for even as the bread and wine nourish us physically, we can at the same time feed on Christ, the living bread, by faith in our hearts. In its origins, the Lord's Supper expresses the truth of God's commitment to the material world in a very moving way. Jesus didn't inaugurate a rarefied ritual with lace tablecloths and silver goblets. The memorial feast for his visible and desperately physical way of dying used the standard, everyday foodstuffs of the ordinary people of the Middle East in his day: a loaf of bread and a jug of wine. We need to get away from the religious other-worldliness and starchy formality of many communion services and back to the basics of a real meal with friends, with enough bread to chew on and a decent glass of wine.

The simplicity of the Lord's Supper in the way that Jesus originally gave it to his Church is an eloquent enactment of the truth that Jesus took on real human flesh and died a real human death. Our God is not afraid to immerse himself in the earthy realities of our everyday life. Even so, the Holy Spirit's availability to believers is not confined within a narrowly religious or spiritual section of life. Just as our sacred meal is the staple diet of middle-eastern peasants and not some exotic kind of temple gastronomy, Jesus and the Spirit both engage with every dimension of human existence.

Life in the Spirit includes the integration of Word and Spirit and a preparedness to learn from past generations, but we also need to recognise that true spirituality includes the active use of the mind and a clear understanding that God is committed to the physical, bodily, material dimensions of human living. If God wanted us to serve him and love him as disembodied spirits, he would have made us that way. In all these areas we need to learn that holy living is integrated living. We need to learn to apply as widely and creatively as possible the resounding words of the marriage service: what God has joined together, let no one divide.

12

The five R's of life in the Spirit

Whenever Britain's schools hit the headlines, politicians and educationalists start to debate whether we need to return to the traditional three R's – reading, writing and 'rithmetic. When it comes to life in the Spirit, there are no less than five R's that the Holy Spirit is able to bring to the Church.

(i) The first R is Repentance
The Spirit of God is the Spirit of holiness. Since he never comes to us devoid of his holiness, he always convicts of sin and calls us to purity of life. He is also the Spirit of grace who reveals the love of Christ, so his work of bringing sinners to repentance is no good reason for the pious gloom and misery that plagues some churches, where believers experience the unremitting drudgery of a life under condemnation. There are however no spiritual short cuts, and a church that plays down the need for repentance will not go deeply into life in the Spirit.

(ii) The second R is Renewal
When biblical teaching about the need to be filled with the Spirit and the availability of spiritual gifts began to be recovered in the historic denominations, those involved were initially described as participants in neo-Pentecostalism. It was not long before the preferred term became Charismatic Renewal, which has more recently tended to be abbreviated simply to Renewal. There are two essential foundations to renewal. First, a clear explanation of two key biblical principles: being filled with the Spirit is a universal

command and not an optional extra for Christians who like that sort of thing; and the complete range of spiritual gifts is still available from the Holy Spirit to equip and strengthen the Church today. Second, there needs to develop within an individual or across a congregation a pressing sense of personal need: an environment of self-sufficiency and complacency is unfertile soil for spiritual renewal. In other words, believers must be helped to understand their biblical inheritance in Christ and must also come to recognise their personal need to be filled with the Spirit.

Many churches have found that it is helpful to have a visiting team from a church that is already established in renewal. If such a team comes to introduce the concepts, there may be little immediate fruit. But if the local leaders have already laid a foundation of teaching and prayer, the ministry team's task is to help the people cross the threshold from theory into practice and the visit can be very exciting and fruitful, with many asking for personal prayer. How far a church can advance in renewal is critically dependent on its leaders. Just as a river cannot run higher than its source, local churches are severely restrained in renewal if the leaders hold back and fail to give a lead themselves in exercising spiritual gifts and demonstrating personal openness to the Holy Spirit. It is not enough to permit some members of a church to dabble in renewal behind closed doors. A church that is convinced of the biblical mandate to be *active* in renewal needs to be committed to every member being filled with the Spirit and exercising their spiritual gifts, not only in midweek groups but also in the main Sunday services.

(iii) The third R is Restoration

As renewal wells up in a local church, appropriate structures need to be provided to assist, sustain and harness the power of the continuing flow of the Spirit. Jesus used the picture of new wine needing new wineskins, and the new wine of the Spirit has often put to an exacting test the old structures of church life. While few people would go so far as to suggest that the New Testament provides a rigid blueprint for the detail of how the Church is organised, many would recognise that the essential guiding principles are clearly outlined. Within the local church, the biblical norm is team leadership. At Antioch the team was made up of prophets and teachers (Acts 13:1-3). Leadership teams in the New Testament are usually described as

elders, using two Greek words interchangeably – *presbuteros* and
episkopos (e.g. 1 Tim. 3:1–2; Titus 1:5–7). Local church leadership
is therefore neither in the hands of a solitary individual, nor left
to the 'ordained clergy' – such terms and a priestly understanding
of leadership cannot be found within the New Testament. There
is no suggestion that such eldership teams were elected by local
churches, and their appointment seems to have involved, at the
very least, a significant measure of consultation with an apostle or
his appointed representative. We know this because when Paul first
planted churches he avoided the premature appointment of elders,
but later he instructed Titus to visit the churches and appoint
eldership teams (Titus 1:5).

The principle of team leadership within local churches is now
widely accepted. There has been less consensus concerning what
have been termed the Ephesians 4 ministries: apostles, prophets,
evangelists, pastors and teachers (Eph. 4:11–13). Some have resisted
strenuously the suggestion that all five of these ministries are still
available today, let alone advisable or even necessary for the
well-being of the Church. Here too the consensus seems to be
shifting. Increasing numbers of evangelicals have come to accept
in recent years the continued apostolic ministry of the secondary
kind that I explored in chapter 8. That is, there are certainly
no foundational apostles to be found today, with the equivalent
authority of the first apostles, but there are continued ministries of
vision and direction, leadership and teaching that involve oversight
of a number of local churches.

Today it is by no means only the new churches that are
talking about the need for apostles. Anglican and Baptist leaders
have also been suggesting that their bishops and superinten-
dents need to be released from administrative tasks in order to
fulfil an apostolic function. It is however doubtful that trans-
local ministries would be credibly and effectively apostolic simply as a result of renaming traditional denominational leaders
as 'apostles'. Once it is accepted that apostolic ministries are
still valid and needed today, then different denominations and
streams need to work out how to identify and recognise those
that Christ is raising up to the distinctive role of apostolic
leadership within, or in dynamic tension with, their particular
structures.

(iv) The fourth R is Refreshing

It was the apostle Peter who coined the phrase 'times of refreshing . . . from the presence of the Lord' (Acts 3:19). Refreshing brings a rekindled awareness of the divine presence, but in such privileged periods of abundant blessing the Holy Spirit does not actually do anything that is substantially new. Rather, he does what he has always done, but with a new intimacy and intensity. Christians experience the promises of Scripture written into their lives with a startling immediacy: we actually experience in the present moment the love of God being poured into our hearts (Rom. 5:5), and what it is to be filled with joy unspeakable and full of glory (1 Pet. 1:8).

We should avoid paying too much attention to secondary reactions such as weeping or laughing, falling or shaking: despite the fact that they may be initially eye-catching. While the manifest presence of God in power can be expected often to provoke strong emotional and physical responses, what matters infinitely more is the hidden work of the Spirit in the inner depths of our being. The biblical Church in a time of spiritual refreshing is like a tomato plant in a greenhouse: developing in the normal ways but with an almost startling acceleration of growth and fruitfulness.

(v) The fifth R is Revival

By revival I mean both the re-invigoration of the Church in holiness, truth and power and also the awakening of thousands of unbelievers to saving faith in Christ. Although no two revivals in church history have ever been identical, all have this much in common: a thoroughgoing dependence on a sovereign outpouring of the Holy Spirit and a radical commitment to sacrificial obedience, seeking to win as much of the world as possible for Christ. Long before charismatic renewal or Pentecostalism, evangelical Christians and unbelievers in revival after revival have experienced awe before the manifest presence of the Spirit of God, so real that he can almost be touched, not only within meetings but even out on the streets. There were days during the Welsh revival when the trams failed to run in some towns. People were so overcome by the presence of God that they fell to their knees in the streets, and if they happened to be praying between the tram lines, the passenger service ground to a halt until the sinner had found peace with God.

The immediate evidence of revival is a rapidly rising tide of conversions. Revivals have the potential to impact the whole of society, leading to a decline in the crime rate and new initiatives in social justice as godly standards sweep through a nation. Revival is not in the hands of human beings, nor is it merely a grandiose way of describing an evangelistic mission. When God has moved in revival power the impact has always vastly exceeded the best of human endeavours in evangelism and social action. (A much fuller exploration of refreshing and revival can be found in another of my books, *Prepare for Revival*, Hodder and Stoughton, 1995.)

So which of the five R's does the Church need at the end of the twentieth century? If we are to know the fullness of life in the Spirit, we need no less than all five! When Claire and I visited Niagara, we took a trip on the world-famous *Maid of the Mist*. Our little boat pressed up close to the falls until we were enshrouded by curtains of mist and the waters' deafening roar. As the deck lurched violently beneath us we felt beneath our feet some small measure of the energy unleashed in that massive surging of water. This gave us the most vivid impression of the outpouring of the Spirit of God in revival power: a mighty and continuing torrent that catches us up and sweeps us along in the love of God; an irresistible outpouring that brings unbelievers to conviction of sin and then to living faith in Christ; a flood of living waters that invigorates all those believers who are pleased to stand in its path, restoring our first love for Jesus and releasing new vitality of faith, carrying us to new depths of surrender and new heights of joy.

Don't limit the Holy Spirit to a small and safe portion of personal blessing. Life in the Spirit can lead us into all truth, not only in our minds but also in living encounters with the love of Christ, bringing repentance and renewal, restoration and refreshing, and ultimately even revival. Please God that he will have mercy on his world so that the two-thousandth anniversary of the birth of Christ may be marked by the Holy Spirit being poured out upon this godless generation in nothing less than full-blooded revival power!

Come, Holy Spirit, and breathe upon us the life-giving breath of God, that Christ may be greatly glorified across the face of the earth. Amen.

Appendix – Guidelines for prayer ministry

I am including these guidelines that I prepared a while ago for our local prayer ministry team. I am certainly not suggesting that they represent the only way to provide responsible pastoral supervision for ministry teams, but I hope they may at least provide some useful starting points for other local churches who wish to provide such guidelines.

As the Lord continues to pour out his Spirit upon us, these guidelines are provided to help us pray effectively for one another. Remember, our priority is always to meet with God, not any particular outward response.

1) Sensitivity is a key word. We need to be sensitive to the Holy Spirit, his work in the person receiving and his prompting of those praying. We also need to be sensitive to the person receiving prayer.

2) Pray with eyes open. This is not only helpful in order to catch those who fall over! You can also observe any particular response as you pray. You can observe the beginning of a work of God, in tears, laughter or other symptoms. If you are not making progress you can also spot when someone would like the ministry to come to an end . . .

3) Touch must always be appropriate to the age, sex and personality of the person receiving prayer. Sometimes it's best not to touch at all.

4) Don't try too hard. Only the Spirit of God can work at depth in someone's life. There's never a need to force any kind of reaction. *Never* try to help God by pushing – it would only hinder.

5) This is God's work, not ours, so there's no need to become over-intense. Relax, and let God work in his way.

6) Don't be over-directive. That is, don't tell someone how you think they should react.

7) Be careful when praying for those you know well that your knowledge of their circumstances is never confused with a word of knowledge. It is wiser to present a divine insight indirectly than to impose a personal opinion as if it were a word from the Lord.

8) Encourage people to keep soaking in prayer, whether they are standing, sitting or resting on the floor.

9) Gentle movements of the hands are symbolic of praying for God to move in someone's life. But there is no need to become a human windmill, flapping around in an excessive and distracting manner.

10) If someone falls to the ground, stay with them and keep praying for a while.

11) A Scripture or a simple phrase used in a prayer will often unlock the heart for a deep work of God. Don't strive or feel under pressure to deliver such words. Trust God, and let him bring something if he chooses.

12) Much discernment is needed over when to pray for more and when to pray for peace. In some people a vigorous reaction is wholesome and a sign of deep release and empowering: to pray for more increases the work of God. Others may simply be worked up, or even using a strong reaction as a defence mechanism: to pray for more may increase their reaction, but not assist any deep work of God. Those with more experience in prayer ministry and counselling may occasionally step in to pray for God's peace.

13) If you ever feel out of your depth, call on someone more experienced for assistance.

14) On a few occasions we have arranged for someone to be taken to another room for help, when the leaders of a meeting have

concluded that his/her response in public was unhelpful, both for him/herself and for others. Such disruptive symptoms could result from attention-seeking, psychological disorders or demonic problems.

15) In the public arena of our services and prayer meetings, there is much to be gained from men and women praying for one another. However, for a variety of reasons we will often encourage a third person to join in. Outside the marriage relationship we strongly advise against such one-to-one ministry between men and women in private. In the public meetings a simple rule applies: if you are sexually attracted to someone and you are not married to them, *do not even consider* getting into in-depth prayer ministry with them.

16) Because God's resources of love are infinite, encourage everyone to come back and receive more, including both those who feel untouched and also those who may feel almost overwhelmed by an intense visitation of God.

17) Keep receiving yourself. Anyone involved in prayer ministry should ensure that they are also being prayed for on a regular basis. Once is never enough. If we stop receiving, we will soon become unable to give very much at all.

18) For some people, anointing with oil brings a release of love and healing.

19) There's no automatic technique or formula. The same Holy Spirit comes in many varied ways, as the stream and the flood, the dove of peace and the blazing fire. All we can do is to ask the Lord to increase his work.

20) Often I take half a step back and pray for someone quietly in tongues. In this way I am interceding for them under the prompting of the Holy Spirit. Sometimes I will then receive a Scripture or prophetic word. Always I am seeking to give them space to make their own response to God.

21) Occasionally the singers or even the recorded tape will declare some words that are just right for the person you are praying for. To try to force such connections every time would be pointless. But be ready for when it happens.

22) If a married couple or members of the same family fall to the ground beside one another, it can be good to link their hands, praying for God's abundant love to bless them together. It is also often helpful to pray for a married couple one at a time, so that each is free to make their own response to God.

23) Some people easily become self-conscious, whether about their lack of response, or about a new or unusual manifestation. Try to put them at their ease as much as you can.

24) If someone wants to confess sin or recommit their life, ask them to pray first (not necessarily aloud!) before you pray for them.

25) If someone is very inhibited, they may struggle against their own stiffness and control. Ask them whether they would like you to pray that Jesus will break them free.

26) Low-level deliverance ministry can take place in a discreet way during prayer ministry. If you face the possibility of something more powerful, ask for help without delay.

27) Many needs are dealt with directly in prayer ministry, under the power of God's love. Acute needs will sometimes benefit from a follow-up appointment with a member of the counselling team.

28) Prayer ministry must always be confidential.

29) The bare minimum that we want everyone to receive is the knowledge that they are loved personally both by God and by us.

30) If you want to grow in this ministry, ask someone more experienced if you can tag along as an apprentice, observing, being ready to catch if necessary, gaining 'on the job' experience.